Everything Forgotten

THE CONVERSATION

Sir John Hawkins

LifeRich Publishing is a registered trademark of The Reader's Digest Association, Inc.

LifeRich Publishing books may be ordered through booksellers or by contacting:

LifeRich Publishing
1663 Liberty Drive
Bloomington, IN 47403
www.liferichpublishing.com
1 (888) 238-8637

ISBN: 978-1-4897-0585-3 (sc)
ISBN: 978-1-4897-0586-0 (e)

Library of Congress Control Number: 2015918634

Print information available on the last page.

LifeRich Publishing rev. date: 12/04/2015

Preface

A time ago, the human race was intelligent, vibrant, creative, and strong – willed specie. Ignorance was viewed as utter stupidity and was not erroneously celebrated as flamboyant creativity. Without television, people were forced to use his or her imagination and frequently passed time with studying to further knowledge. See, knowledge was sweet nectar, honey to a bee; today it is sour, a mere repellent to a society in desperate need of sweetness. Society has divorced knowledge along with deep conversational thought and has leaped into a promiscuous lifestyle of illiteracy, vague superficial perception, and hollow-vein conceit. As humans, we have forgotten everything that once made us the thriving, competent, and illustriously peculiar people we once were.

Our specie, in past times, strived for luminosity; we hoped for a brighter future; our present was filled with hobbies conducive for all humanity. History was defined through art; music and creativity was the essence of linguistic capability; education was something people would die in attempts to achieve; which was its nutritional assorted fruit of true supernatural power. Everything was done out of one complicated, often misguided and often misinterpreted word, LOVE.

Out of love birthed so many different ingenious ideas and logic. Love was once a way of life, an essence readily defined by human behavior. The love of conversation is gone, the love of true precocity is lost and benightedness is now the normality of an under achieving and yet overly accepting society. The love of moralistic character is overshadowed with superficiality and selfishness. True companionship and longing for one another was built on the strong principle of love which is now replaced with microwavable lust drenched with insecurities which leads to lewdness; it's sickening. The love of self is substituted with the love of acceptance; we are a society built upon the thoughts and idiotic notions from one another. Because of this, society has rejected individuality and has now taken on a frivolous collective thought process that has led to everyone mimicking one another in a childishly negative way. Love was accepting one's difference which gave earth's individuals the confidence to be his or herself and to seek positive regard from not only one another but from within. Simply put, love was the sole influential phenomenon that motivated society to actively experiment, listen, build, create, revolutionize this being we call life.

To prove that love is and should be our main motivator to live and to experience life to its supernatural fullness therein, I quote Paul, as he wrote these words in 1 Corinthians 13:

If I speak in the tongues of men or of angels, but do not have love, I am only a resounding gong or a clanging cymbal. If I have the gift of prophecy and can fathom all mysteries and all knowledge, and if I have a faith that can move mountains, but do not have love, I am nothing. If I give all I possess to the poor and give over my body to hardship that I may boast, but do not have love, I gain nothing. Love is patient, love is kind. It does not envy, it does not boast, it is not proud. It does not dishonor others, it is not self-seeking, it is not easily angered, and it keeps no record of wrongs. Love does not delight in evil but rejoices with the truth. It always protects, always trusts, always hopes, always perseveres. Love never fails. But where there are prophecies, they will cease; where there are tongues, they will be stilled; where there is knowledge, it will pass away. For we know in part and we prophesy in part, but when completeness comes, what is in part disappears. When I was a child, I talked like a child, I thought like a child, I reasoned like a child. When I became a man, I put the ways of childhood behind me. For now we see only a reflection as in a mirror; then we shall see face to face. Now I know in part; then I shall know fully, even as I am fully known. and now these three remain: faith, hope and love. But the greatest of these is love (1 Corinthians 13:1-13, NIV).

It was love. Whether you believe or choose not to believe. It was love that created not only originative ideas, inventions, creative thought, art, music and so much more but life itself. Enjoy as you read beloved brothers and sisters.

Acknowledgments

I just wanted to personally give my gratitude to everyone who has supported me and encouraged me to go forward with this project. It has long been a desire of mine to share my thoughts and to share a bit of who I am and what I believe to be MY truth. Thank you so much to those who have accepted me, took time to learn about me, and those who have come to appreciate my unique sense of being, without judging me based on my outer exterior.

To my sons; Sir John II, Prince Jireh, and Czar Cassi Hawkins, daddy loves you guys with all his heart. You three are the best things to have ever happened to me. You are responsible for my maturity in Christ. I thank you, I love you and this script is for you; I pray you read it one day and remember what being a Hawkins is all about. Be a Man; one who commands respect through your behavior.

To you... L'CN☺

Grace of peace

FOREWORD

Look around and see that times are changing.

The way we once thought is of the past; the way we think now can be considered questionable cognition and proves to be to our decline; and the way we will think, as time passes and society grows older, will be as total and utter inconsiderable people. The problem is the way we think ultimately translates to how we behave. Our very perception on life and our perception of self will cause society to fall, we will crumble, we will flat-line and then we will die because our expectations are inordinately inferior to what we once were. Our minds have influenced our lack of respect for not only one another but again, ourselves. How did we get here? When did our self – fulfilling prophecy begin to decrease and turn negatively against ourselves? Women are not demanding respect from men; men are not demanding respect from women; families are disorganized as to how we should operate and there remain questions about particular roles within the home, while the patrons of society are becoming more and more ignorant; totally incapable of holding enlightening conversation. It is a travesty!

Look at the cover of this book again.

The cover displays the reality of the state of affairs in our society. Although our past is full of wrong doing to one another racially speaking, intellectually we are on the rapid decline. The image of the cover suggest that as the book is titled "everything forgotten," we once thought with a full mind; full of intellect, full of conversation, full of ideas, full of forward movement. As time passed, we became foolish in our own minds, slowly forgetting everything that once made us civilized, slowly forgetting that which set us apart as people from animals, forgetting everything that made us unique and yet thriving. We stopped expecting and started accepting. The picture on the cover of this book tells the story of our past, present and future state of comprehension, intellect, respect, and overall, wisdom and love; it is a picturesque of who *we were*, who *we are* and who *we will become.* Just look at our youth today, enough said. We are steadily on the decline and this book will explain to you who, what, when, where and how with the hopes of a Social Revolution.

Grace and peace

Chapter 1

Ladies and Gentlemen?

(THE PENIS ARGUMENT)

Socialistic interaction proves that times have changed, are changing, and will continually change; and based on factual evidence seen from day – to – day reciprocation; this kind of change is not for good but unfortunately bad.

The history of MEN

Allow me for a moment to share what would now be considered history; a great tale of tales, an apologue of honor and patronage. Once upon a time there was a strong and decent specie that were not perfect by far, yet nominally responsible and loving which was displayed by their sacrificial deeds. This specie went out from the hut day to day, working and providing for his woman and offspring while instilling discipline, principles, restructuring his dwelling place behavioral trends, and inspiring confidence in his matron. He was head of his haven, prided bread winner, and ultimate decision – maker; this specie were mighty in every way imaginable. He was revered, loved, and trusted. The abode took pride in him and he in his. This specie, boys and girls were historically known as, yet universally forgotten, MEN. Yes, historically speaking, men were proud; men were dignified; men were measured by his keen ability to provide and his willingness to sustain his house in every way conceivable. Men were, at one time, able to multi-task. Today, this short, yet factual soliloquy is out of date; now historical in nature, a myth of an ancient society. REAL men are now nothing more than a fairy-tale.

The degradation of manhood today

Today, men are the reorganized and reaffirmed women of yesterday. More and more humanity is witnessing a shift in the tides, the waves are rising, and those rising waves are drowning manhood. Now what we have washing upon the shore is the replacement of testosterone for a man concealed, feminine induced, estrogenic placebo which has fooled men into submission; men today can be defined as the women of yesterday. This day is filled with non – working, irresponsible, chivalrously deceased boys who seemed to have tucked his penis between his legs. He now behaves through the influence of the stench of his infectious, worn, and diseased vagina. He is wearing his pants around his backside showing his underwear like a woman displays her thong, he wears trousers resembling that of denim type paint (they're called skinny jeans today again displaying his curves like a woman) and is as flamboyant characteristically as ever, seeking the attention and acknowledgement some women would seek. Need more be spoken?

Written in the excerpt "Godly Men: Head or Tail" are shared thoughts of the state of men in today's society. Check it out:

Godly Men: Head or Tail?

Will the real Christian brothers please stand up? Wait; are there any real Christian brothers out there? Optimistically, I want to say yes, and in my heart I believe Christian brothers do exist. However, pessimism sinks in, and we are becoming increasingly difficult to recognize. So, the bigger question is why are we hiding? Does not the word of God say that we are the light of the world? If the light doesn't shine, how can this world of darkness fully illuminate? Men of God we have to stand tall and firm; it starts with our own families. Notice what is suggested is our OWN families; meaning stop judging others when you yourself have chinks in your armor (deacons)!

Men of God, why are we not working? We are allowing our help mates to provide for us when we are to provide for her. Our wives should be supportive of us, but not by providing for us. Stop! I know what many are thinking, money is not all we are to provide; how about spiritual leadership, discipline to our children, emotional support, and tender love exemplified through our actions. Why don't we love our wives as Christ love the church? Why are we demanding respect and submission yet we haven't submitted ourselves to the salvation of God which reciprocates the love of Christ through us to our Wives in our own homes? Men of God, well, Men period! STOP ASKING FOR GODLY WOMEN WHEN YOU YOURSELVES ARE NOT GODLY MEN AND YOU YOURSELVES DON'T ACCEPT MANLY RESPONSIBILITY!!!

Know your role

God has made us into the spiritual compass for our families. We seek God first and His righteousness (Matt 6:32-34, NIV) and He gives us insight as to what direction we are to embark upon. God gave men direction in Genesis from the very beginning. For some odd reason, many believe had it not been for the fall of man, men would not have to work. Even in God's perfection He gave man a task (job). As men, we were responsible for the upkeep of God's blessing, which was the Garden of Eden. Why have men forgotten about this fact? Why are our women being forced to endure extra duties to accommodate the homes WE reside over? Let me put it to you this way; our women were given to us as helpmates, not primary resource providers. Look at what God says through His word about man (Adam).

The LORD God took the man and put him in the Garden of Eden to work it and take care of It (Genesis 2:15, NIV).

We were given the duty to work even in the beginning. That scripture says nothing about women doing the work, yet we (Christian brothers/

men) allow them to take on the full mantle of OUR duties. Men of God, with all due respect, MAN UP!

Note: Now, allow me to add to this; if there is a reason for you not to work due to physical ailments or agreements made between you and your wife that is your business. I am speaking to the lazy brothers who sit home and do nothing (no housework and or offspring duties) to help the wife who is working.

Directionally, we have the responsibility of leading our family toward Christ. In doing so, we must know our roles in the home. We are the priest of our household. When have you ever seen a lazy priest? Such a thing doesn't exist. A priest is constantly at work. We were not commanded to sit back and allow the wife to head or reside over us (the same is true of the church). God uses the example of marriage and family to describe our roles not only in the family, but the body (church) as well. We are too apt to allow the women to lead the way. We should not be demanding any form of respect, submission, and or authority when we ourselves have not accepted the role God has given us.

[As a side note; men of God, please stop allowing your wives to stir up trouble in the church and abroad please. In love, correct her (not publicly) by instructing her in the ways of the Lord. Christ does not want nor does He appreciate division that is caused by some of our wives gossiping and carrying on; be a man]

Simply put, get a job, know your place, and MAN UP!

Head over your ultimate responsibility

Christ has entrusted to us our wives. He has given us the ultimate responsibility to care for them but we have run from it. So when a woman is running you and your house you are saying "I am not the man God called and EVE I'm following you, I'm not man enough, and you should take the lead for me." Remember this, God called David a man (yet he was still a boy) after His own heart. A man after God's heart has no business taking the back seat while cowardly neglecting his responsibilities. We have the nerve to say first; wives submit! How dare we request such a thing when we have not lead through love? Consider what happened in the garden; we audaciously put the blame upon Eve when God put us over the garden and gave instructions on what we should and should not eat.

> And the LORD God commanded the man, "You are
> free to eat from any tree in the garden; but you must
> not eat from the tree of the knowledge of good and evil,
> for when you eat from it you will certainly die (Genesis
> 2:16-17, NIV).

As you can see, Eve didn't come into creation till after this command was given. God gave Adam the command because Adam was the overseer of His (God) blessing that was the garden. We can't blame Eve for our inability to accept responsibility gentlemen. Today, this is still a debate because men will not accept responsibility for what man (Adam) did. To this day, we are still blaming the women for our insecurities, character flaws, and overall, OUR sin. Just like Adam, God commanded us but we submitted to Eve instead. We do not have to continue in this way men.

If you want to be the head of your house men, you must first head over your ultimate responsibility. God instructed wives to submit to the husbands but He gave us the ultimate responsibility as leaders, to love our wives as Christ loves the church. Truthfully, wives have the secondary responsibility in submission to a Godly man. However both are required to obey God!

> Husbands, love your wives, just as Christ loved the church and gave himself up for her to make her holy, cleansing her by the washing with water through the word, and to present her to himself as a radiant church, without stain or wrinkle or any other blemish, but holy and blameless. In this same way, husbands ought to love their wives as their own bodies. He who loves his wife loves himself (Eph. 5:25-28, NIV).

I find it astonishing how men are quick to quote Ephesians 5:22-24, yet they stop there. Again, we have a problem accepting our responsibility. If we are going to delegate responsibilities, let us start with ourselves. Just like judging others is not our jobs, we are reminded to continuously examine ourselves. By doing this, you are actively cooperating in God's plan for the family. You can't do this with your own strength (trust me, I've tried and failed in my own marriage), but only by the power of God (His spirit) who is made strong only in our weakness. Men; to love a woman (especially a black woman - no offense) require supernatural strength and wisdom, items of which we have none within us, but in Christ alone, we have it all.

Verse 25 of chapter five illuminates the sole responsibility of the husband. Christ tells us to love our wives as Christ loves the church. As we know, loving people period is difficult, especially when they hate us. Imagine Christ only loving those who treated Him justly, who liked Him, or better yet loved Him. The same grace and mercy that sustains us should sustain our wives, as well as our children. The time is now for men to realize we were made in God's image, so we are expected to emulate His likeness in all things. This is why we were given this command, from the beginning it started with us (man). In Adam we fell in Christ we were/are raised. The actions that we exemplify must be that of Christ' love for the church, a successful marriage will display, and or be the result of a husband's love for his wife. The commitment we share with Christ will illuminate in our wives. (Thus, we are the light of the world).

Christ had to decrease so that we might increase. Let me explain, He walked among us (filthy sinners, i.e. decreasing) to fulfill the law because of our inability so that we might have everlasting life (hence, increase). So men, as we selfishly love ourselves, remember in the same way, we show love for ourselves by loving the part of the flesh that was *united with us in Holy matrimony. Men of God, we have got to learn to love even when we are disliked, unappreciated, disrespected, unjustly treated, and yes, sometimes even unloved. We show our obedience by taking on the Character of Christ, presenting our wives (justifying them) as blameless, radiantly gorgeous and blessed (thus-a Proverbs 31 woman resulting from having an Ephesians five type man).*

Men, when we do this, more than likely, you will not have to ask, beg, or demand respect. Just as a sinner repents, so does the wife when she realizes the blessing that is you through Christ. First men, we have to MAN UP! If we are the heads, understand the task; we give direction and seek guidance from the One who saves. We take up our own cross and follow the Creator of all things. We love because He first loved us, this is OUR responsibility.

Lastly, understand this, Christ was and is the Head but at times (as scripture points out) He allowed Himself to be treated as the tail, but ultimately established His kingship (the head) in His humbled heart to make us (all sinners) blameless in His sight. As men being created in His image should we not also rule through love and yes sometimes humility (Selah)? So ask yourself men, are you a man representing the head or a man comfortable being the tail?

The aforementioned excerpt queried to all men, not just men of faith but to ALL men. Are you comfortable with being the woman of the relationship? Are you okay with being the helpmate? Based on the evidence, one would have to conclude that men are indeed comfortable with being losers to his own cause. However, full responsibility must not be imparted to men alone, but women must take at least a percentage of the blame for the fall of real men. Yes, chivalry is dead and men are responsible for its untimely death. It must be stated however, that if men killed it, women provided the lethal dose for men to inject into chivalry's veins.

The Dying Essence of Her Gender
(THE VAGINAL ARGUMENT)

So much can be said of women today. Today, the women's rights movement is visibly depicted amongst society. Women are more outspoken, making more money, are in management positions, taking care of home, are outwardly more aggressive, more prideful, extremely more dignified and well, women are what men used to be before the movement. Now, some will ask or assume that one believes that there is an issue with this. One would argue against the women's rights movement being an "issue" BUT would suggest that since the movement, has lost a certain magnitude of allure to her essence. Allow an explanation as this statement can be taken fallaciously.

The movement was righteous in its cause to seek equal treatment for ALL women. Women should have a voice, should share in decisions and if forced to work to provide for a family or self, should earn that of what a man doing indistinguishable work earns. However, the obstacle it presented was and is that it took the woman from her home and she, once raised in a way forgotten to mankind today, has failed to teach her own daughters in the way of a real woman. Woman of that day were able to care for a home, while taking care of not only herself, but her offspring as well. In the southern region of the states, women were taught in the ways of southern hospitality, self-respect, meal preparation, housekeeping, mother-hood and far more important, the ways of Christ and a woman's expectations therein. These functions were conducive to the family and character building of a woman. These responsibilities were depictions of the LOVE a woman shared for her husband, her offspring, and most of all and more importantly, her God. These actions taught more than service to a women but it also, when taught correctly through a motherly mentor, taught self-worth and self-respect.

THAT WOMAN IS

Graceful, merciful, Spiritual, visual, beautiful, yet so much more

All that and a bag of chips with Kool-
Aid on the side, the red kind

So much ambition locked up inside, a being of
light so small, yet so tall, aged in experience,
yet not too golden— we call it fine wine
So much potential as to what will become, hope I'm around
to see your success with each seasonal passing of time
The lure of your beauty, the curves of your ...
shhhh!!! Won't disrespect you, a woman sublime

Graceful, merciful, Spiritual, visual, beautiful, yet so much
more

Known imperfections make you perfect in all of your ways
Not speaking of God's perfection; of course no one
can ever compare to our Lord, the Ancient of days
Your knowledge is sexy and your intelligence
is noticed, even upon a simple gaze
You are bound for greatness and Godly success
is situated deliciously upon your plate
Take, eat, and remember Thee ~ as
this bread and wine you taste

Graceful, merciful, Spiritual, visual, beautiful, yet so much
more

Ridiculously talented in multiple areas of life ~ you are
wonderfully made in such a way that in you comes life

The new Eve of mankind – only this time,
Eve's not easily sifted – she's just right
Powerful enough for true submission because
she realizes her duty to the Christ
A motherly, caring, nurturing individual
The presence, shear essence, so pleasant to
speak with, comfort and stability is appreciated, in
your conversations comes delectable insight

Graceful, merciful, Spiritual, visual, beautiful, yet so much more

The basis for this entry is to encourage you to see it through
"It" is you, be you, seek Him, who created you,
for His glory, give Him His just due
Be exciting; be educated, beautiful and outstanding
Never let anyone or anything stop you from withstanding
The pressure to, yes pressure, oh the
pressure that comes in being original
Be spiritual, revelating, breath-taking,
goal-obtaining, oh-so exhilarating
Fly in what you call your "swag" never
lagging in your confidence
Let your wings spread
Take flight, you're right for the vision; talented,
out-spoken & beautifully gifted

Graceful, merciful, Spiritual, visual, beautiful, yet so much more

In so many different ways, the woman of today lost her self. A mere assumption is the movement had a hand in it because it took mom away from home and placed her in places away from the secure home she built. When mom was spoken of, children couldn't attach non-spiritual, immoral, party-going, social networking, promiscuous, selfishness, imprudence and irresponsibility to her name! No, not by far could any of those adjectives fit what defined or described OUR mother. On the contrary, mommy was, kind, smart, beautiful, respectful, selfless, sacrificial, loving, nurturing and mature beyond her years. Most of society would define mom as being highly regarded, respected, and overall her offspring's security blanket. An excerpt written by an actual woman entitled, *"What is a Real Woman"* says this about R.E.A.L women:

WHAT IS A REAL WOMAN

So you want to know just "what makes real a woman?"
Well to best describe this wondrous and most marvelous
complexity, I must begin with what she "is not".

A true woman is not ashamed or afraid to admit when
she is wrong, even when she is not. A true woman is not

against or opposed to giving 110% to balance out the 90 that her man may sometimes be forced to give. A real woman is not embarrassed or enamored with the fact that she is not the size 6 that parades across the television, but a healthy and voluptuous size 12 that prowls across the bedroom. A real woman does not become the 6 in public to tear her husband down, but becomes the w (think about it) in private to make him feel like the warrior he is. A real woman does not tell her children, "do as I say, and not as I do", but does as she says and becomes an example by what she does. A real woman is not defined by the Cashmere on her back, or the Prada on her feet, but by the calluses on her hands and the powder (baking that is), from cleaning and cooking to make sure her family is well taken care of.

So you wanna know what a true woman is …..First of all and most of all, she is GOD fearing. She recognizes the fact that through Christ she can do all things for this is her strength. She accepts and supports her man for not just the person he is, but what he will one day be in Christ. She provides and supports automatically. (I got your' back baby) She loves and gives unselfishly (sometimes to a fault). She defends and protects her family fearlessly (say what). She corrects and chastises tenderly (I love you). She worships wholeheartedly *standing next to her man. She worships brokenheartedly (but still worships), when he does not care to.*

So you want to know what a real woman is. Well,.... she's just that........R.E.A.L. ......Respectful.... Enticing...Accentuating...Loving...this is what makes a real woman.

Without that security blanket women and men have uncovered a more IN-secure character and have a destructive way of viewing life because mother is/was too busy away from home to give those most valued lessons of yesterday. You know those lessons, how to dress properly, covering up and leaving some to the imagination; never allowing yourself to be disrespected by any man and knowing your worth has fallen on deaf ears because mother's may be saying it aloud but not completely displaying it though her behavior. Mothers and Fathers used to teach on how to approach a woman and how to receive gentlemen. Women taught girls the difference in knowing when she was being respected and or courted properly and when she was being disrespected and treated as product. This lesson too, has fallen on deaf ears and or is not being taught anymore. As a result, a rant written *"Game, and the Women who fall for it"* years ago explains the state of the woman today and what she deserves from the lack of respect she has for herself.

Game; And the Women Who Fall For It

It is ferociously enraging and bewildering to understand the social dialogue which transpires between a fiercely attractive woman and a well - groomed (sometimes, most of the time not), ego - maniac of a guy. As he tells her things that mirror's language of a rampant buffoon, she listens attentively, admiring the words flowing from his un-nerving, idiotic, stereotypical, and worse uneducated speech. The most lethargic yet confusing feeling of disappointment overcast my heart and dampens my soul as she (the woman being gamed) opens her mouth to share her seven digits with him for more of his child-like quotations and hidden agenda through conversations. As I sit there in disbelief, my mouth is wide open and my face is flat as the table I write on. I ponder this scenario over and over in my head and what I determine is this; women who fall for the stench of his essence deserve the heart ache he may bring. It also makes one question her education and self-esteem level. Like I said before, Game; and the women who fall for it, how sad is this?

What is Game

It is important to point out to the audience that this is by no means a hate session on the men involved in such behaviors. The text is a way of sharing what game is and the type of women who like to play it.

The question still remains. What is game? The definition of the word which comes from the Mirriam-Webster Dictionary is compelling. The noun version of the word is "an activity engaged in for diversion or amusement (Mirriam-Webster Dictionary, n.d.)." Initially this definition was more than enough to make my case. However, more definitions from that very same dictionary captured mine eyes. "A procedure or strategy for gaining an end and an illegal or shady scheme or maneuver (Mirriam-Webster Dictionary, n.d.)." These definitions are interesting to say the least. Still there are a couple more that are needed to be seen before I present you with the metaphoric definition of the word itself. The word "game" as a verb means to take dishonest advantage of; according to the Mirriam-Webster Dictionary.

Captivating is the word one would have to use after reading these definitions. The definitions exude the personified usage of this term and its immediate danger to every woman under its influence. Look at the verb definition of the term. "An activity engaged in for diversion (Mirriam-Webster Dictionary, n.d.)." In this phrase the word diversion speaks the very truth of the metaphoric usage of the word "game". Usually, when a man has to fling various amounts of compliments to a woman he gazes upon for the first time from a far, one's first thought is this guy has something to hide. The initial words to start a conversation from a respectable, honorable, and educated man should be nothing more or less than; "Hello, how are you today?" The problem with the aforementioned approach is this; it is a dishonest one! The man is hurling praises toward the woman as a smoke screen to a male hidden socialistic and erotic agenda. The words flowing from the man's mouth are to engage in "flattery" in order that the woman is thrown off guard by his "smoothness" that will utterly cloud the true essence of his insecure ability to speak eloquently. Simply put ladies, the "game" coming from his mouth is a cover up and it would behoove you to understand that his words have not ANY substance.

"A procedure or strategy for gaining an end and an illegal or shady scheme or maneuver (Mirriam-Webster Dictionary, n.d.)." Wow! To "game" is to essentially have a strategy to win. Take basketball for an example; if the coach wants to win a game, he or she will implement strategies (plays) that will come in handy while increasing the possibility of success. What am I saying? I am simply advocating the truth that to a man who "spits" (communicates with game), a woman is a game; a source of entertainment. Moreover, the definition points to two words that solely define the metaphoric phrase. Scheme which means trick is what these men are using. The man is tricking the woman to believe that he is sweet, loving, honest, and caring. While tricking the woman, the man is using the second term in maneuvering his way into her mind, hoping to penetrate her heart by giving birth to new thoughts in the mind of this woman of his self that are drastically untrue.

To sum up the controversial subject with all the aforementioned information mentioned above, one would have to determine the definition of the urban usage of the word "game" to mean the falsely artistic and linguistic skills a person uses that lacks substance to shield away from the hearer the truth of who the person really is and the motives the person secretly possess for a social and erotic relationship between the two individuals involved. Surprised, upset, disagree, if this is you obviously you are a "gamer" or a person "gamed." In this world, humanity is described into two categories; the predator and the prey.

Wishing upon a star

The poem "Pure Symmetry" defines a woman from a time ago, a type of woman that is becoming more and more extinct daily.

PURE SYMMETRY

The truth about her essence is not
that she keeps one guessing

It's the fact that upon one gaze, one is amazed,
as to how the presence of her openness has made
a way to eliminate one who may be stressing

She's not about the outward display
of ornamental grace

For her, the inward justification of what
she stands for in moral taste is more
important than flaunting her waist

Size or her voluptuous breast; she's
convicted in making man fall into lust

Confidently she's proud of what Christ blessed
her with and Honors Him by taking that which
he made so perfectly and covers it up

She flirts not, as she understands
the underlying disaster that could
unintentionally inadvertently become

Her maturity is shown by wise choices in
NOT making herself a citizen of this world
and the cultures activity to succumb

Instead, her mind is on being a model; a
true beauty on display for Christ and not
man so she repents from the world

Faithful beauty is what REAL men visualizes
when they stare upon her - she's far from a gem, to
us she's a rare dazzling and harmonious pearl

She's like a diamond in the rough as this world
has been proven to have jagged edges

She stands firm and smooth, passionate
about spiritual matters, to her husband -
loyalty and trustworthiness she pledges

She's set apart

She sounds perfect but instead her allurement
is found in the fact that perfect she is not

She's not a hypocrite, she doesn't display something
of a lie, and her moral character is one of correction
from the word of God, her conviction can't be bought

Her desires are of her husbands; she has no shame
in admitting she's married to the Christ

Her behavior's evidence; she gives herself away -
by not speaking death but instead speaking life

Imagine a glamour that speaks the adorning
and aesthetic truth within her conversation

For this beauty presents no gossip, slander, reality
television or what's going on with the next celebrity
man or woman from her shared information

Instead - she share's intelligence, passion,
she speaks art and debates so exhilarating
with her activists like stance

Refinement is blooming with each word that
is spoken; she leaves the world in a trance

Knowledge is true power and she
shares it with great romance

Her elegance is celebrated, but again, it's
not because of her outward appearance

She blessed with pure beauty

Men everywhere knows and accepts that
she has been claimed by the one man

God has sent her way, she's quick to shoot down any
thought or any plans of another man's advance

She removes all obstacles because she believes
Christ blessed her with a family

Something so real, so true, she's convinced
of its road toward eternity

Courageous is she to submit to who God has
given to uphold her dazzling beauty

Because she understands that it's Christ to whom
she is really submitting to; it's her duty

The family is charming and it is due to her
tireless efforts in which she performs

The many admirable tasks of being a mother
and Wife she represents her family well;
through her they're placed on a platform

Through her are adjectives and verbs of
strength, elegance, wisdom, and confidence

For she is the epitome of beauty and
worth every moment that was spent

In her creation, because to the world she
has proven that Christ exist eternally

For she is the definition of what an artist, a
creationist would define PURE SYMMETRY

She's simply beautiful!!!

Praise be to God

A woman of character, strength, notable worth, spirituality, self-confidence and self-respect is what the poem displays. This type of woman is dying. Today, face-painted, cleavage showing, gossip drenched, intelligence lacking, conversationally challenged, reality television viewing, social acceptance seeking, crowd pleasing, no self-respect having, half-witted, worth lacking, non-loyal, morally corrupted women are the ingredients which leads to a hellacious, ominous main feature to a healthy meal. Today women are just ornaments on a dying tree. A woman's speech today can be equal to or less than that of what is shown on Nick Jr. A five year-old has more to add to a conversation than that of a woman these days. All the face paint, tight clothes, and lewdness in the world will not and cannot cover up the fact that women today are pretty much on the decline. Women today are unfortunately defined only by the anatomical difference of gender; she is merely defined by what she possess between her legs; nothing more. A plea for real women today are just as prominent as the one for real men to return to his and her places in history.

How disappointing, especially the young woman of today and her inadequacies. Her lack of responsibility and the promiscuous nature in which she behaves is simply troubling. The most bewildering thoughts cloud the mind of one who sits in awe over where womanhood has gone today. Today's mother is leaving her children with strangers so that she may go out and indulge in behavior's laudable to today's standards which is licentious in every way. The mere conversation of a woman today is befuddling; it is in that conversation that one realizes the ignorance that becomes her. She simply knows nothing, cares for nothing, seeks anything but sadistic type superficial praise and attention, she is simply nothing worth having. What a sad occurrence we as a society has witnessed of the last 10-15 years and going. What a shame. Today is the curse of a new type of woman...a worthless type.

WHO'S THAT GIRL!

All my life I've experienced all kinds of women
Women I was raised by and women who had my head spinning
All of their names I can't recall
Some were special and some not at all
The females who meant the world to me
Were usually the ones who made me hurl internally
Funny how we consume that which is harmful to our bodies
Causing our insides to decay similar to the result of too much caffeine on
our teeth

The first girl I encountered; her name was joy
One glimpse at her and you'd understand the name
However, her name was nothing more than a ploy
See I came to realize the joy she gave was my painful shame
Beauty on the outside, externally a knock out
I was involved in things I never knew existed
Joy was inherently evil but her grasp was
sealed like the bag called Ziploc
Tried to leave several times yet she insisted
I stay with her and endure the sufferings

The pain felt good I can't lie about it any longer
Kept my head down, away from sunlight, she
was my dark cloud just hovering
Years of this and I built strength to leave when I became stronger

The second girl I experienced; her name was certainty
Met her on the phone without months of visual
No surprise she was the cause of much ambiguity
Kept my interest however the relationship was suspenseful
Same old story; she abandoned me
The story ends comically without much fussin
With her; the only certainty was she wasn't for me
Oh! Did I mention she left me for my cousin?
Not much to tell or reveal in this story
It ended badly and yet she still wants to befriend me
Never before uncertain about my family
Until I met my girl again her name was certainty

The third Girl – her name was pleasure
Unfortunately pleasure was known for her bedroom knowledge
I didn't realize that one day I would attempt to make her my treasure
Still tried to wife her even though she had mileage
She was kind, sweet, and she did have education
Her heart seemed pure but I could see it still aches
She was my first trial at physical stimulation

Hated to be another experience for her that added to the possible shame
to her face
In her pleasure she brought much pain
The two were synonymous with one another as so it seemed
Sadly Pleasure was stuck in her old ways
In my trying to make an honest woman out of her I found that with her,
only the Lord could redeem

The last girl I will discuss, her name was stupidity
She was the one I let get away for something
that I knew wouldn't last always
She was my joy, my happiness and my peace
In her I found true serenity and felt love
would follow us throughout our days
She was the one who-in me-spoke ambition
She shared with me her tragedy - showing me her trust for me was real
However, in my stupidity - I never thought
what we had would come to fruition
Even though her true love for me-through her actions were revealed
Bewildering, defines my state of mind during that time
Cognitively lacking common sense to grasp what God presented
Thinking back with heartaches wishing I would have made her mine
But instead I was an idiot, my low self-esteem cost me
a happiness; in my stupid decision I relented

Her name was everything and I now have nothing!
She was the one God sent to define me as something
All I know now is my unfailing yet deafening curiosity
Her name is my pain, her name is/was
forever will be known as stupidity

Everything about a man and everything about a woman is vastly being forgotten. What our society once represented in times past is no longer. A new wave of imposters are being born and living right under the noses of those of real authenticity. Now, this chapter is not to say that there are none left of any worth but to illuminate this dying breed of once known and valiant people who now suffer under the suffocating rule of these ignorant and superficially motivated genders. The question now resides within the reader. Are you amongst the forgotten or are you the stench of humanity polluting this new era of mankind?

Take a moment to pause and start the conversation. Will this next generation produce the historic man and woman?

Chapter 2

peer individualism

Socialistic interaction proves that times have changed, are changing, and will continually change; and based on factual evidence seen from day - to - day reciprocation; this kind of change is not for good but unfortunately bad.

Individuality has come and gone, as seemingly, everyone in our environment seeks to identify with one another. Peer individuals are the new individualist of today. What is peer individualism and how can one identify him or her? Peer individuals are those who claim to be individuals but are shaped by what his or her peer group thinks, says, or does. In an adolescent approach, he or she seeks social or peer reviewed acceptance to feel comfortable in his or her surrounding environment. So, these persons' are merely peer individuals; people defined by others believing to be actual originals. These days are filled with individualist becoming collectivist in a feeble minded attempt to become a part of the "in crowd." The majority are dumbing down his or her intellectual dialect to speak with uncultivated, beguiling purpose for the sole intent of becoming "like them." The majority are leaving behind modesty and accepting a more flamboyant approach to everyday life and it is and can be seen in the way he or she dresses, sounds, thinks and or behaves. Things have become so bad that one cannot identify the majority from the stereotypical minority. In a bereaved attempt to become a part of the "in crowd," our society is losing ground in the areas of creativity, innovation, and dexterity. The excerpt *Description of Me* is indeed what this society is missing:

A simple description of me:

Calamity meets peace; yet peace meets that
which is rambunctious in the natural
Respectful of those which are labeled dreadful
because in reality we're all quite sinful
In a sense – I am a liberal
Dispositional attributes that cannot be altered by any human being
Embedded into this body, it was all part of the
plan, or should I express - "grand scheme"
Enlightening – yet fiercely frightening; be careful upon approaching
this, it's always a two way street – or better yet a mystery

Retro in approach-respectful in purity-a true
founder of the term and phrase chivalry

Angered by ignorance-driven by purpose; shameful

of belligerence yet, so overwhelmingly weak

Patient to a point - loving of the truth; a superhero

to some; superman with no booth

Caring of humanity, damning of self-vanity - blunt

in what is spoken – a liar who craves truth

Eclectic by choice – choosing to use voice to speak life to

those who displays death through emotional instability

Electric characteristic – personality too strong, still a

witness of the gospel through deed or through song

So many words to describe, a personified type scribe

An activist of the people, who are incapable of a good ole fashion fight

Artistically, resoundingly and suspiciously troubled by sanity

Seemingly wise until it comes to this man

and the affairs of him personally

Lured by kindness; his features are subpar

A simple compliment is something shut down faster than a sports car

Socially updated to the point of activity

Outrageously associated within the confines

of self-destructive promiscuity

Yet not defined by a freelance of sexual relations

Speaking of the indiscriminate acceptance of

everyone without underlying discrimination

Bound to service, as a life without ministry is seen detrimentally

Testicles are huge – by this, is meant boldly

outspoken in linguistics and in actions

Perseverance is key – an individual totally driven by passions

Those passions are plenty but the time is few in availability

To complete the task – so frustration resides in side of this personality

Insanity is seen as normal as it promotes freedom of expression

Schizophrenic traits outside of mental suppression

is viewed as subjective weapons

Objectivity is keenly repressed as it is damaged by the memory

Drastic change is expected yet still inherently rudimentary

Viciously optimistic for others ~ visualizing the best is still yet to come

Dangerously pessimistically inpatient when it

relates to the opportunity of freeing love

Rules are despised as are those who hunt for the weak

Talents galore – "jack of all traits" master of

none still realizes the blessings

Open to receive from others words of wisdom

Closed to receive from others negativity that creates

longevity of things that are quite dumb

Impossible to reject short beginnings and where one comes from

Hyperactivity increases with thoughts of being

used to increase Christ's kingdom

Erotic in the true sense of the word imaginable

Fighting urges daily to do what comes so natural

Feeling like a fiend you can refer to this being

as lector - first name Hannibal

Saved this attribute for last because it's depreciated not casual

Can't help the desire that burns; this being is just so sexual

Explicitly warranted – can't help but to

crave that which is so pleasurable

Part of the personality flaw – characterized as defile able

The mind bleeds thoughts of perversion that are just unfathomable

People define it as being freaky – yet in its

true sense, still held accountable

Uncontrollable lust, like blood thirst from vampires; it's not sustainable

What can I say; I'm misunderstood in my complexity

People tell me to appreciate what God has created; it's true beauty

However, I see it as a curse; scriptures call me an enemy

Yet, I can't deny my ways and views are that of true CREATIVIY

I GUESS I AM WHAT THIS WORLD DEEMS, CREATIVE?

Individuality & Originality

Individuals are a dying breed and originality is decreasing daily. Will the real individual please stand and be proud? What is individuality anyway? Before anyone reading this is offended and debates rather or not he or she is an individual or original, let us first explore the meaning. David G. Myers, author of *Social Psychology* states, "Giving priority to one's own goals over group goals and defining one's identity in terms of personal attributes rather than group identification" (Myers, 2008), is what one would deem individuality. True individuals are not socially motivated by being "liked" or accepted; meaning, individuals identify his or her self from what Myers called self – concept (2008) in which a person answers his or her own question, who am I, instead of relying on the "in crowd" or the desired social environment to define him or her.

With TRUE individuals, there is not an issue of knowing one's self and there are no social comparisons. An individual, TRUE individual will not allow self to be compared or grouped with any social group rather, take pride in being different and remains original. With a TRUE individual, he or she could not and would not allow a group to subliminally, metaphorically, physically, or moralistically define him or her. While it is not assumed that everyone is seeking validation and or social acceptance (*I am not saying that everyone involved in social media is, but there is a majority*), one would not have to find validation or seek attention on social media sites if he or she were true individuals. As a matter of fact, those not seeking acceptance and a need to feel connected have no use for such an atrocity which many would say, defines social media today. One cannot be defined as an individual or an original if the aforementioned descriptions fit the one claiming to be what he or she is most definitely not!

The poem *Rejected Acceptance* illuminates this opinionated observation:

REJECTED ACCEPTANCE

Damning evidence suggest that we no longer seek the
FATHER'S acceptance; our behavior suggest that we
live life not for the SON but for the social relevance

Facebook, twitter, text message, my-space; we seek
social attention far more than we do HIS FACE

WE STAY

On our phones, lap-tops, ipads, and computers; flirting
with sin, girls, and guys who desire to prove you

Are nothing of substance but another sad and
ignorant statistic; of another young person
or individual seeking social acceptance

**We give ourselves to social media as prostitutes gives themselves
for gratuity; openly breaking the first commandment, putting
friends and family before Him who is the creator of humanity**

More of our time is spent sending lines than fervently
reading the very lines that saved us; we rely on the
information highway but in God we don't trust

Salvation through obedience is a secondary notion; primary is
our goal to seek enlightenment through another's emotion

The system is corrupted and no one seems to be paying attention

We're born and we live, we live to be accepted by the very people
or persons who enslaved everyone one of us; our behavior is
mirror reflections of these people whose aim is still to shame us

We seek to look like them, so we change our look surgically or
by viciously hiding our beauty with paint resembling asinine
clowns, they continue to mock us; they feed us lies, telling us it
will make us feel better about ourselves and we fail to see that
they're trying to mask us; hiding our true identity of individuality
through being made peculiar by His sacrifice; the aim is to get
us to resemble them in order that with them we may also die

We are born with pride and culture but we surrender
it to fit the very culture that they set in place; which
is public drunkenness, lewd behavior, even common
sense, we substituted dignity with disgrace

Spiritually we've committed suicide just so we can live our lives as
those who are the "socially accepted;" If you pay attention you'll
see the malnutrition within yourselves you're spiritually neglected

You haven't eaten

We're afraid to stand out for the one whose brought us
out – we fear the criticism; from cynics of this world this
proves we openly practice paganism; how can we be called
the sons and daughters of the most high; when we've given
up the truth of God's word to mimic Satan and his lies?

The truth is the world and the ruler of the air can care-less
about your being; truth is the goal is to get you focused on
these worldly things; And what does it say that you rather
look and behave like openly defiant heathens; I guess
you'll see the day of judgment when the words "away from
me, you evil doer, I never knew you" finally sinks in

Believe it or not, originality leads to and is conducive to
individuality. What is originality? Originality is a concept foreign
to the world today. In a world where music that is produced
is looped and copied from music years ago, proves that there
is a dying and real extinction of originality. Daily, people are
prancing around proclaiming to be originals. When in reality,
originality is fading daily due to the decrease in creativity;

creativity is and is born of TRUE individuals. People today are not a fresh breath of air; civilians today continue to prove to be the convoluted mess that pollutes our environments chances of re-birth and regeneration.

The Webster's dictionary defines originality as "the power of independent thought or constructive imagination" and another definition states "freshness of aspect, design, or style". Examine the first definition of originality and what we have is individuality defined. "The power of independent thought," is what the definition states. People aren't thinking as individuals any longer. Unfortunately, people are so concerned with identifying with others that original thought, original speech, original dress, original conversation; original behaviors have fallen by the waist side. The need for social acceptance has raped society of originality. Humanity is now left with a watered down version resembling that of flavored water, of individualism.

True originals created that which we studied for years. True originals were those who revolutionized this world with his or her uniqueness and brilliance. True originals brought flavor to this bland and tasteless world. Think of the commercials displayed on television today, the reality shows, the music, the face book pages and conversation, the tweeting, the attire worn today to attract (leaving nothing to the imagination), the night clubs, the social clubs and fraternity's; again, society has turned back to its days of tastelessness. Without originality, society is headed right back into a type of social depression (for the few originals actually living today). What the world needs to return to prominence and a place of worth are the TRUE originals, the revolutionaries that brought society so much creativity, flavor, and excitement. We need Vincent Van Gogh back, we long for the return of Beethoven, Stan Getz, The Roots, we desire Bach to return, we crave Monet, we want Gustav Klimt, bring back Maya Angelou, bring forth Picasso, we want Cornelius Eady, where are the Langston Hughes' of today? The poem *Speechless* illuminates that which this society is not any longer. One of the issues is society speaks too often but with great quantity comes a lack of quality. True and real individuals understand that sometimes speech is overindulgent at times.

SPEECHLESS

If you don't have anything nice to say,
don't say anything at all!

Many times over, I've heard these words
My mother's stern look as her gaze prompts a turn
In direction
My intentions - were to say
something that would burn

To murder the conscious with a few adjective
describing nouns that would lead to stern verbs
Processing information is with me, done differently
So many vigorous yet vivid thoughts,
my brain waves seize repetitiously
Overwhelmingly, I've learned to control my
tongue to a certain point in controversy
So I find it better to remain viciously
outspoken; but I do so silently
Venomous poison spewed ravenously
through me cognitively
Sheppard's thoughts that squeezes the
human confidence crucially

Often times there really is no need to speak

I find peace in the silence the mind speaks
Being quiet allows one to learn more –
so it's fitting educationally
Silence is comfortable - in that it doesn't
force a conversational piece
Instead it is like a realm of protection, so
I call silence my fortifying security
In tranquility, I can live a life of peace
No noise – means no drama – no drama
means life is at this certain time...easy

So I don't speak overtly, rather
when I do decide to speak ...
I make sure it's done so in importance, intentionally
The problem sometimes; people speak too much!
Saying things that hold no substance, speaking
of non-sense with illiteracy hot to the touch
Proving that no brain is within them
Or the brain is damaged severely starting at the stem
Speaking of things, that has caused humanity,
to decrease in terms of their I.Q. and in
knowledge we've lost our minds literally
What ever happened to enjoying another's company?
You know, that comfortable speechless moment,
that in which your heart thumps aggressively
just from the presence of another being;
They say its comfortable silence in one company

*But why should I talk if peace of mine is
not yours to receive at that moment*

Instead, I decide to quiet myself
Not trying to be mysterious or to live a life of stealth
The truth is, prayer is done in silence, lest
one looks like a crazed individual

And if this sparks silence, then it's obvious that
we should all be quiet, as prayer in this world
is something desperately needed...it's critical
I choose not to speak!
Shhh...

COLLECTIVISM = CONFORMITY

People of today in the westernized culture have adopted a collectivist way of living; psychologically speaking. How ironic is this, that a culture built upon individuality, which brought forth individualism and thrived because of it, now seeks collectivism socially. What is collectivism? Again, according to David Myers, collectivism is "giving priority to the goals of one's group and defining one's identity accordingly (2008)." Simply put, collectivism is giving one's own desires, in this case of the book, one's own moral, cultural beliefs, spiritual beliefs, character, personality, and well, individuality in order that he or she may fit within the confines of the group he or she desires to be a part of. Again, today, everyone desires to look the same, sound the same, and behave in the same manner; the exact kind of world that socialist's dream of.

Here is the problem with collectivism in today's society. Collectivism, as a socialistic idea, was never meant to be the way civilians today display it. Collectivism is really a socialistic governmental ideology used primarily in the Eastern portion of the hemisphere. Collectivism is a type of socialism used by the Chinese and other Eastern European Countries to control people and their lives within those Environments. There are pro's and con's to collectivism, but that too is another conversation. The way in which collectivism is spoken of today is equal to and not greater than the word, conformity.

Myers states "conformity is a change in behavior or belief to accord with others (2008)." Rather than being adults, the civilian population is folding to mere peer pressure, accepting that in which he or she, outside of the group, would probably never accept alone. Simply put, **TODAY'S SOCIETY AND THE PEOPLE THEREIN HAVE TOTALLY SOLD OUT TO FIT IN!** People have forgotten how to be themselves, how to be individuals, how to be unique. What saddens more is that people cannot recognize or realize that he or she has indeed sold themselves out as slaves to a lost generation of vain conceit and lewdness. Somewhere in the middle of time, people desired to identify. Once people started identifying, his or her identification came by the ideology of others rather than self. Even the bible speaks against conformity. Romans 12:2 states, "Do not conform to the pattern of this world, but be transformed by the renewing of your mind." The pattern of this world speaks volumes to everything aforementioned in this chapter. The pattern of this world again speaks to the way individuals have accepted moralistic change within his or her self to fit the mold of society, it speaks to the way society behaves and is adopting this world's thought process.

You can see conformity everywhere. We have forgotten who we are as individuals. We have forgotten how to be ourselves. Who are you? You answer that question, don't allow anyone else or any group to answer it for you. Ladies, take it easy on the make-up, it was only created to enhance beauty and to decrease age, not to be an everyday costume of prostitution (Not saying that is what you are doing). Some of you resemble clowns and look very fatuous (I am sorry, it had to be said) it is just too much! Men, pull up your pants and loosen your jeans, you look like females. No one wants to see your genitals bulging through your trousers or your underwear, it is not attractive and that is not cultural. Honestly speaking, who are you?

Whatever is true my brothers and sisters always be exactly who you are, don't fold to peer individualist.

I am...mE!!!

Startling emotions, my brain's experiencing
intense commotion
I can't seem to wrap my head around this calamitous notion
This maniacal thought which deteriorates
worse than that of erosion
Slavery is aborted, so to tell me to remain in chains is subject
to relational conflict which fails to impedes character explosion

I am a black man
Blessed, **L**oving, **A**ttractive, **C**harismatic,
and **K**inetic, and I will withstand
All ignorance of any man, who tells me to
"dumb it down," NO I WILL STAND
I will not sit upon command
My ancestors broke through those chains of
shame before I stood upon this land

I am a free, black human being
Ferocious, **R**espectful, **E**ducated, and **E**rotic and will never be
A person who disguises my intelligence for another's
confidence to remain high in velocity
YES, I CAN READ
I won't hide that fact, so the corporate world
can feel less intimidated and at ease
I am braided up, swagger styled, strong
willed, and limitless in ability
I will not be muzzled by those who can't
handle yet want to tame me
I am courageously
Out of your realm of fear, you don't have to employ me
Keep your jobs, relationships, and personified ego that believes
That I have to bow down to your socialistic agenda just to BE!
NOT IN MY HOOD, PLEASE!!!

I am a proud, black, and free individual
Prestigious, **R**ooted, **O**utstanding, **U**nderstanding,
and **D**electable, I know you want a taste
You want me to change my appearance
so I can be less appealing in a way
Which elevates, you because your confidence, in
the mere presence of mine has seen better days
Sweet is the taste
Of this dark chocolate, you want to create
Something sour like you because not only am I
outstanding in appearance but I'm able to educate
I devastate
People like you because my stature is
appealing to your romantic mate
Which pisses you off more, my sexiness, or
the fact that I actually have a brain?
And might I say, MY, WHAT A BRAIN!

I am one of Faith, who is black, free, and proud
Fruitful, **A**ppreciative, **I**nspired, **T**rusted, and
striving to be **H**oly, I WILL NOT HIDE
Who I am for a job or individual I strive
To be a better man, which DOES NOT, include
me suffocating the Spirit that resides
Inner me, enter me and you'll see that inside
Is zealousy to be who Christ called me to, I rise

To the occasion I will not quench what burns within for a ride
In luxury, I will never be, what you want me to be
DESPITE WHAT YOU THINK, a true CHRIST lives in me
I'm not one who delights in games, a real
black man doesn't play hide and seek
Don't tell me to be something I'm not,
because my desire is to represent HE
The creator of all things
I will not deny HIM for a piece of the AMERICAN DREAM
I'M JUST ME
AND WILL CONTINUE TO BE
NO DEMON IN HELL, EARTH, OR CORPORATE
CAN EXCHANGE WHO GOD MADE ME TO BE

AND ONE LAST THING
HE USED MY ANCESTRY TO FREE ME FROM *SLAVERY*!!!

SELAH!!!

Let us converse on this chapter. Are adults folding under peer pressure? Are you one of them and aren't able to recognize it? Are individuals, TRUE individualist, people of past times?

Chapter 3

Fallen Harmony

Socialistic interaction proves that times have changed, are changing, and will continually change; and based on factual evidence seen from day – to – day reciprocation; this kind of change is not for good but unfortunately bad.

Real music has deceased and society is responsible for the dagger plunged into the lungs of its essence. So much aggravation and explosive resenting anger describes the emotions when speaking of the corruptive, erosive, and non – melodic racket society has to suffer through today. The trash offered today as music should be burned at the stake and pierced through the hearts (if there was one) of those who manufacture such enormity. Music was laid to rest probably about a decade or two ago with the emergence of the supposed "hip hop culture." Along with the hip hop culture came the decline of enlightenment. Once the hip hop culture started to emerge into the mainstream sickness of popularity and corruption, it seemed as if every other genre of music lost its marbles as well; in obvious competition with this new phenomenon called hip hop music. A time often forgotten of is when music was actually an intelligent apparatus; a voice to those who had none; a definer of emotions; a conversation brought forth, through at one point, love. Music was everything and everything was in music. But with the death of music came a new era of human stupidity, ignorance, superficiality, selfishness, and well, everything forgotten.

AFFLICTED MELODY

You were created to represent something naturally beautiful; now you're all made up to fit today's society poisoned by corrupted influence your essence is tainted, for us you're no longer a mate suitable; to represent those of an eclectic intelligence; we reject you and leave you to this tragic civilian crowd of ignorance!

Wounded by demand, the people have spoken

A strong system, manufactured by citizens yet morally corrupted, it's clear the system is broken

Your intentions were to reveal a wide range of human emotions

An outlet for those who created you; only now
he or she is influenced by the token

I used to love your harmony; once beautifully
orchestrated, it now sounds like commotion

Intellectually driven, lyrically enlightened, I identified
with you before ignorance caused your erosion

You've alternated your being just to fit in;
upon you our faces are cast down

Make-up doesn't make you look more attractive;
on the contrary, you resemble that of a clown

No one takes you seriously; you're
nothing more than a gimmick

A side show, an abomination, a disease turning
terminal and it's only one way to cure this

Return to your days of glory where strength
was revealed through your cords

The natural sound of talent which stood alone, uniquely
driven through poetic thoughts manifested in words

Your resonance was at one time multifarious but now it's universal

Universally and unilaterally deficient, your
mere existence has become worthless

Cognitively pacifying, you calmed the long and gray days

In the midst of trouble we turned to you to fervently
explain what we couldn't find the words to say

You spoke for us and through us you were made

To bring about adult conversation, peace,
collaboration, now humanity is in disarray

You were faithful and loyal; mankind looked to you
for guidance as you communicated through love

Your new found licentious ways has found us
in shame of claiming you, we're done

You sold out just so you could sell out to the
thousands of the same people who mocked you

We stood in support as they fought to change you
and stunt your growth; their illiteracy blocked you

From total enlightenment you were once deemed excitement

Now to all with any sense looks down
on you with disappointment

*You lie through your lyrics, your pitch and
melody sounds like kid jingles*

It's painful to listen to you now; a pain worse than shingles

We fear you are lost and so is this new generation

*They'll never know how you spoke for
us in countless situations*

*They'll never know how you were able to proclaim love,
describe fear, elaborate on real sexual stimulation*

*How you offered release, defined despair, concern,
gave voice to our anger and elation*

*You were once our thoughts, feared to be
spoken through uttered communication*

*You stand a distant memory – something historic
in nature as you near saddened extinction*

Alas, real music has become an art of past times

The last breath draws near as you ... FLATLINE

The increase of ignorance and the constant decrease in
discipline has lead humanity into this time of misfortune,

disconnection, and well, music that cannot be digested. Mankind is no longer seeking higher education and respect, but rather coin and overindulgence; this has led us to the very dismal explanation of music today. A time ago, music was composed out of pure mastery and creativity. People in "those days" were seeking to enlighten the world with an art form unfounded to mankind. These individuals were flaunting the God given ability to connect and communicate in an artistic and yet climatic way. These individuals allowed the music to speak volumes of his or her skills. The music of that day screamed of staunch intellect, grace, and passion like none other. Today, society is damned with illiterate fools throwing around nouns, adjectives and verbs to causes of none but to fill his or her pockets, while a society obviously lacking intelligence, seeks to bless this mess of noise and racket, posing as musical talent by giving it (music) undeserved voice.

In times past, music gave hope, defined our state of mind, and lifted the weight of life's issues off of our shoulders. A drive home from a long hard day at work was blessed with the radio playing tunes that would ease the pain of the day. Music had the power then to allow us, although but for a moment, to escape the harsh and cruel reality of life. When we didn't know the words to say, we would spin a record. When we didn't know what emotion to feel, some talented individual would explain our thoughts and feelings through his or her chords accompanied by talented voice. Music spoke on behalf of mankind and the hope therein. Music was the voice of reason and logic. Music was our super-hero and our will to live past our miserable existences. Think about this; when you were down, what did you turn to? When you were head over hills in love, what did you rely on to share in the emotion and to explain something that was, at that time, new to you? Weddings, funerals, churches, graduations, all forms of celebrations and events were blessed by music as one that gave voice to the occasion.

As it would be today, the morons of the music industry are no longer interested in presenting authentic harmonious pleasantry, but rather, rhythmic noise to stimulate the over-sexual night clubs and under-stimulated minds of this era. Since money subjugates reason, dexterity and skill, and while sex is bartering the media integrity and substituting love of music for lust of currency, the music industry will be forever influenced by the dying societal minds of today. Because of this the music industry has pulled the cord on an art form previously already on life support. The industry has proven not to be interested in educating and presenting quality. It would seem today the main focus of the industry is to distribute quantity that strongly opposes knowledge and insight accompanied by talent. Therefore the industry has to claim responsibility for the crap associated with the word, the idea, the history known as music.

The industry itself can be pardoned a percentage of the blame for its offerings; the industry does only what the people of this world request. The music industry alone is run by people whose interest is only to please the public eye (or in this case, ear). The public today proves to be driven by superficiality, lust, promiscuity, and selfishness; the public has no love for substance, no, the majority of the public have become egotistical, self-pleasuring party goers with shallow and vein perception. With the decrease in morality, character, education, individualism, and love, comes the fatal decisions made by the industry on a day to day basis to push garbage and pawn it off as treasure. This brings the idea aforementioned in this chapter, hip hop. Check out these lyrics excoriatingly speaking the reality of the so called *"hip hop"* or formerly known as the (rap) industry today.

TRAP GAME

The rap game is trapped fame

A silent death to the craft came

With the emergence of the now defamed; and

ignorant driven genre of what they explain;

To be musical talent drenched in shame; called the rap game;

What a shame;

We've gone from; lyrics that spoke of life

To lyrics that speak nothing but unadulterated lies

We've gone from; once heralded as poetry

That which this day screams of laudable abhorrent stupidity

No real intelligent person is listening

Break the chains

You're thinking you made it but you know not

You are on display; they have trapped you by their plot

To keep the ignorant deep in ignorance

And they are doing this through what

you celebrate as your sick lyrics

You've been had! In your veins they

have injected this stimulant

It's called you, you're the ignoramus

And you went along with it

Be ashamed and break the chains

You sit in it

The feces you've created and demanded that we take a whiff

Like a dog, you've been trained to sit

Like a slave you submit

To them; the very people with a clever plan to

keep out of their realm of intelligence

What a shame

The longer we waste time chasing currency

The more time they have to cover up conspiracies

They have us caged and locked away like wild beast

Yet we put on a good display; YES, it is

you performing for your treat

All of this to ensure we never walk amongst

them; they do this to keep us out their seat

They do this to keep us under their feet

Break the chains

Use your gift; if you have one to speak the truth

Use your strength from your ancestral

blood line and loose the noose

The longer we hear about all your cash and your hoes

The less our community hears of injustice and of societal woes

(Towards your community)

Use your voice and let the government know

Put down the damn Mic if you are not willing to expose

The cover ups that is held right up under our nose

But you don't!!!

You'd rather sit back on your knees and give

them a job with your mouth and blow

The opportunity to educate, encourage and

enlighten – yet you decide to blow the real show

Be ashamed and break the chains

All I'm conveying is this rap game cost you TRAPPED FAME

You're the stain

Somebody pass the Charmin so that we real

people can wipe this crap away!!!

Though the "hip hop culture" cannot take 100% blame for the decline of music, it can and should take most of the blame. Yeah, one can assume the thoughts, "oh here we go, another older person downing rap and saying it is bad for society!" Well, here is the issue with those assertions; 1) I write this as a 30 year old, young Black man who adores music and grew up a rap enthusiast to a certain extent; 2) I don't believe rap is the sole cause of music's death, just having contributed to it through its idiotic artist; 3) I believe real rap music should stay and in itself was a pure art form born of poetic licensure or a spin from poetry I should state. What is meant by the term "hip hop culture" in the sense that it has ruined music is that this new phenomenon has not only claimed the lives of rap, but pop, R&B, neo-soul, etc. The hip hop culture is not just about music anymore. The culture is all about a supposed swag, style and the way one dresses (pretty much the various fads of the moment); the behavior; the way in which communication is relayed and even the human thought process.

Hip hop (or rap as it once was) was not always so stereotypically idiotic. It used to be a skill displayed by those who could actually tweak the English language into rhyming nouns, verbs, adjectives, and adverbs through the creative expression of the individual's inner thoughts and or ideology. Many believe that the true form of hip hop came from the idea of poetry or poetic expressions. Those pioneers of hip hop actually had to be well versed or blessed in the practice and knowledge of the English language. Some artists were actually college attendees or graduates. What is often forgotten about hip hop is that it used to educate, relate, and used often to communicate. What exactly was communicated?

Lyricist, during a time forgotten, communicated pain, joy, wisdom, deep thoughts that brought about conversation, struggle, freedom, and displayed true metaphorical lyrical talent. These forgotten artists like Talib Kweli, Mos Def, Common (the old Common that is), Boogie Down Productions, Digital Underground, Rakim, Public Enemy, Outkast, Naz, The Roots, and a few other artists that exemplified what true lyricist and hip hop artist were. The individuals noted, with a few more of course, was responsible for a yet another musical emergence where talent + education and knowledge = success of another musical metamorphosis. These artists communicated and displayed talent that made hip hop relevant; it was not just entertainment, NO! It was much more than entertainment, we related with these artist, these artist spoke our minds, hearts, desires, and so much more. It wasn't about entertainment; it was about relating and revealing not only the talent black people held but also our education and skills. Now look at where we stand!

Today, hip hop is now a genre in its own. With the coming millennium came a whole new character of lyricist; a flamboyancy rap artists of the past would have destroyed lyrically and clowned publically. No one of this day and age dare face one of those crews or individuals of the past; lest he or she be put to shame. The new millennium did not bring skill and education; it pretty much brought fads, pure ignorance and gimmicks. A rarity it seems these days to have an MC speak of something with relevance or importance. Today, hip hop exemplifies what this society has become. Because society has become so much more superficial, vein, self-promoting, and artificial; hip hop has become the voice, reason, and representative of this era.

Hip hop became too big for its trousers. Because hip hop became a music metamorphosis, it became a huge money maker, everyone wanted to jump on board (for the money of course). Somewhere along the lines, hip hop became a culture that adopted R&B, neo-soul, pop, and now techno dance music. Remember when R&B meant rhythm and blues? Remember neo – soul used to grip us with lyrics that spoke the very nature of our thoughts and feelings? Vivian Green sang to us about emotional roller coasters, Bilal said sometimes he wish he wasn't himself (how many of us has ever felt like that?), Musiq sang of love and how difficult it is, while Jill Scott almost made her listeners ejaculate with her song *"You Love Me."* Angie Stone spoke of how it sucks to miss something you don't have which was love in her song *"Wish I didn't Miss You."*

See, neo-soul is/was music; the lyrics represent what most of society has felt at one point in life. The lyrics to most of neo-souls music can be related to day to day life. Neo-soul also used to use more real instruments in its music. The trumpet, saxophone, trombone, violin, and other real instruments were at least attempted in the music. Yet, even neo-soul is losing in the fight against the cancer that is the music industry as it stands now. Today, hip hop's synthesized noise has replaced real musicians and real music. Sounds are fabricated to sound like instruments, yet the sound of hip hop is often heard in the aforementioned genres way too often, kidnapped by the thug that is the hip hop culture.

Rhythm and blues has probably been, next to rap music, the biggest sell out of them all. Remember rhythm and blues brought us "slow jams?" Slow jams were equivalent to rhythm and blues music. It too at one point used real instruments, but once taken by hip hop, instruments of music became synthesized racket. Even the lyrics changed in R&B. Factually speaking, most of R&B was love songs, sexually stimulating songs, or songs of agony and defeat (Mary J. Blidge for instance). What is forgotten is how emotional music used to be and how it used to. Today rhythm and blues is nothing more than noise and disaster. At what point did lyrics about being in the club infiltrate R&B? When was partying ever a part of that genre of music?

One can actively see how this generation is leading the world into the last days when everything one hears is speaking of raunchy sex after a night at the club with most likely a stranger. What is often forgotten is how love-making was done to slow jams! To prove that times have changed as well as women, instead of making love to the smooth sounds of Boys II Men, Jodeci, or Silk, men are being allowed to pummel women listening to these fraudulent rappers or some form of heavy metal either worshipping Satan (or smacking God in the face - Godsmack ring a bell), or speaking of nothing more than getting his rocks off (how sad). The music today speaks of nothing but reasons why Christ's return is eminent and on time! The day rhythm and blues sold out to hip hop is the day this world started to display its ugliness and lack of humility. We showed that we are no longer in the closet but our inner vein desires and selfishness will be put on full display, along with our lack of intelligence; an idea long forgotten.

What this topic comes down to is the lack of love in not only the lyrics of the music, but the production of it as well. People at one time loved writing music, loved composing it, loved placing the arrangements in order, and loved creating something that impacted people. Lust is the new love of today; it is why divorce rates are sky rocketing to new heights; it is why babies are being born without fathers; it is why most women know nothing but giving themselves in hopes that she can feel something of worth;

it is the reason why this world has been forgotten and we are but mere shells of our ancestor's pasts. Music today without true love sucks!

Let us converse on the matter at hand.

In your opinion, where does music stand? Is music what it once was? Is it better or worse?

Chapter 4

Loving Lust

Socialistic interaction proves that times have changed, are changing, and will continually change; and based on factual evidence seen from day – to – day reciprocation; this kind of change is not for good but unfortunately bad.

HISTORICAL LOVE

A time ago Love was patient, Love was kind
It didn't fail, it would only but last forever as it passed through time
Times has changed and the people along with it
Love is now lust personified; while the truth of it is
now covered with lies and ignorance
A time ago, love was an action word; in school we learned the term verb
Simply meant to take action; as words spoken without
behavior to follow were met with stern
Eyes – as they leaked with disappointment and grief
I'm now stuck in the unfortunate reality

It's like a horrible reality television show
Today I'm asking, is it me? Where did the real love go?

Historically speaking, while I'm stroking this keyboard, my heart is weeping
At a lost for words - misunderstood behaviors arise as
I'm stuck in a time where love was peaking
I remember when love lead to unions that would last forever in a day
Unfortunately love is nothing more than words met with disrespected
behavioral trends that would have casted love away
Love is frowned upon now in this new day and age
It's nothing more than a show now; something to be casted with actors on a stage
There nothing real about it; everyone's getting in on the game
Play with fire and you get burned is what the old people used to say

What happened to the commitment that love used to stand for?
Love used to carry hope; well faith today has gone out the door
I remember when love would never disrespect
It would have never longed for another in anyway because
to love, this act alone would be defined as neglect
There was a time when love was overtly and overly caring
Love is lust personified now so selfishness is the only way, no such thing as sharing
In another's feelings and or what they may be dealing with
Instead love now meets another's needs with neglectful
behavior, harsh words, and frustrated fits
Love is failure now, back in the day, Love never quit
Honestly today, in the face of love society as obviously spit

No one wants to fight the good fight and challenge themselves
Today, true love can only be found in the library on book shelves
Love used to care - but no longer
There was a time when love was everything
It wasn't so painful to love as I'm sure we've all felt the sting

The sad reality is today, everyone who uses this word believes he or she understands the emotion and or notion of this butterfly effect, yet rejects its true existence and the defining responsibility within. The truth is, love has been long forgotten and the meaning of love today has been misconstrued for the actual definition of lust. People just cannot tell the difference between the two anymore. Gentlemen, just because a young lady can make you think about her daily and fantasize about her on the hour every hour doesn't mean that you are in love. Ladies, just because this man is able to captivate you with minimal conversation and display gentleness to you for six months does not make him the spouse you have been looking for. To the ladies and gentlemen, just because the opposite sex can turn you on sexually, on the outer exterior look well groomed or put together, and make you climax in the bedroom, does not mean you are in love. Love is so much more than a night to remember.

Declaring Love (Love Jones)

"Love, a word that comes and goes, but few people really know, what it means to really, love somebody" (Kirk Franklin). Those are powerful lyrics from the songwriter, Kirk Franklin, a man who totally revolutionized gospel music. However these words, these lyrics, are simply stating a truth that is sometimes intentionally and unintentionally distorted. People say I love you all the time, but what does it mean to love? See, often times we find ourselves hurt by what we thought was love but we were too naive, too emotional, and too blind to understand the real and true concept of this phenomenon. We've all done it.

ENDANGERING NECESSITIES

There are some things I require of you
First, I would like your words to speak nothing but the unadulterated truth
Please don't lie to me like you would anyone else
In return my anger in your truth will instead be met with feelings of joy that is heart felt
See when you lie you're saying you don't fully trust me
You only trust me enough to provide smoke-screens to protect me
I appreciate it, but I don't need your protection
No weapons formed against me shall prosper no matter the situation

Second, when we speak, I want you to be nervous
Like I am with you because I don't want to offend the person I adore

Offending you would be offending me and our particular purpose

I want you to choose your words carefully so that in them our feelings may soar

I want to be lost in what you say, persuaded even, in such a way

That I'm carefully hanging on to the verbiage that to me, you relay

Hanging on for dear life

By the excitement your words ignite

Third, can you be delighted in seeing thee

Can you make it your business for your heart to flutter, even skip a beat from simply gazing upon me?

Would you allow your heart to exude elation, your blood to exemplify elevation, your eyes to reveal revelation?

All this from the mere physical appearance that defines my nature through education

If we are unable to see each other for a time

Could we merely press play on our feelings though they were paused during a time of sublime?

I need to know that our movie is everlasting

Not just a momentary, physiological responsive rated X scene ending by ejaculating

Last, is it possible for you to always want me sexually?

If I put on a few pounds will the two still become one flesh biblically speaking

One way I reveal my love to you is through sex scenes

Scenes with inhibition because there's no laws in love-making

Can we explore fully the love we so adore within each other to the core, I'm just asking

Because I desire to make you happy through satisfaction, never allowing anything boring

Think about these things because I'm basically asking if you truly love me
Because love is dangerous and so are its necessities

From the mind of a psycho-socially disturbed being
Sir John Hawkins
"My feelings are seen on my sleeves"

Loving Fantasies

As society continues to stagnate, so does certain terms, words, and ideas. The phrase "I love you," should not, in today's world, be shared from one person to the next. Personally speaking, unless one is ready to prove his or her love through what he or she does and not merely what he or she says, the phrase should not be proclaimed. Before one proclaims something so bold, he or she should be ready to exemplify love's difficult characteristics. Marriages have ended because of the falsifications behind the belief of what real and true love is. One out of every two couples are divorcing today because the two could not display love's greatest and most important attribute; it is not the "feelings," as those come and go, but the greatest attribute which defines love is commitment, the very idea that is lacking in marriages and relationships today.

BEWILDERING UNIFICATION

Misunderstood, misconstrued, and misleading; yet for you and I,
together, new heights we're reaching, achieving and still cleaving

That which is misunderstood is usually
enraging and simultaneously causes fear

Yet, none of that matters as long as you have
me and toward me you are near

From the outside looking in I'm sure we look bewildering

Outsiders couldn't begin to understand; he or she
cannot fathom what we have, it is truly OUR thing

This would perceive us as insane, precarious
and utterly strange in our dealings

Because real and true, honorable – biblical love surpasses that
which this world recognizes; it's far beyond emotional feelings

Misunderstood, misconstrued, and misleading; yet for you and I,
together, new heights we're reaching, achieving and still cleaving

See, men can't understand why I tend to your every need

Why I hurtle over to you when you call; they just can't see

That YOU are ME, how could I neglect myself when together
we're one physically, emotionally, more so spiritually

Men won't fathom the unselfish nature I display
unto you because in this world men live selfishly

Men will not understand why I put you first

How I fill YOUR cup when you thirst

Why no one comes between you and I without being cursed

They perceive my "yes dear" as weak but fail to realize
that's my strength as it is quoted in the verse (Eph. 5)

Misunderstood, misconstrued, and misleading; yet for you and I,
together, new heights we're reaching, achieving and still cleaving

And women can't understand your submission towards a man

See, they fail to realize it was ALL part
of God's design, His master plan

And that your submission to me has little
to do with me – the individual

But your submission is unto God and to the
head of the house within the spiritual

Realm of the house, women can't understand
you or why you love me the way you do

Enraged at the display of love they nash their
teeth; but in repeat; I continue to honor you

While you're preparing my plate, my clothes,
rubbing my head, and caring for my every need

They are in the background secretly meeting and gossiping
inquiring as to why you call me "daddy" publicly

But while they're doing this:

I'm loving you as it is often misunderstood
and spoken ill of in code

Yet it is Christ our Savior who understands our
love and in return he Honor's our abode

Love is so complex that if you ask ten people what the word
means, you're likely to get ten different answers. The truth
about love is everyone experiences it differently. Love has
its necessities; the main fact about love is love is not a mere
emotional phenomenon; if that were true, we'd all be in love
with multiple people at one time (*which I guess is possible yet*

difficult to handle). The fact about love is love is sacrifice. If you are a Christian reading this, you understand what I mean by sacrifice. The term Agape comes to mind; agape being the Greek translation of the word meaning "unconditional/sacrificial love." This unconditional love has no conditions on love and was represented by Christ on the Cross as He lay there bruised, battered, utterly slain, dying for mankind.

Sacrifice is something mankind is incapable of. As humans, the selfishness within us will not allow us to sacrifice something or someone for the enhancement and security of the relationship. What kinds of sacrifices are needed to exude real love? In marriage, compromises have to be forged. Sacrifice is a remedy, a required solution to keep the marriage going peacefully. In relationships, sacrifices must be made in order to keep the relationship strong and headed in a positive direction. WHATEVER your mate, spouse, significant other, asks of you, why is it even a thought (unless of course it is illegal or blasphemous against Christ).

Real love calls for REAL sacrifice; there is no way around it. People need to feel secure, if one is unwilling to sacrifice the nouns (*i.e. person, places, things or ideas*) causing damage to the relationship, questions will arise of his or her true love towards the individual. What are you willing to do to show your significant other that your love for him or for her is real? If the answer is nothing, you are clearly not in love with this person.

You just lust for him or her. Here lies the issue of love, everyone wants to speak it today but will not set forth the necessary behaviors to display its truth.

INSATIABLE CRAVING

It's like the pain a baby experiences when he or she needs nourishments; it's like going without hydration for

71 hours with one hour left to live there's no aqua flourishing; it's like a wolf with a scent of meat in its nostrils;

worse, it's like a drug addict going through detoxification while within his pockets are narcotic pills!

It's painful....

I desire that which is long forgotten
Historical in nature but re-created to mean nothing; yet it's spoken of often

I'm hungry

I desire this everlasting sweet smelling aroma
Today it's a stench but I believe in miracles that this essence is not just a misnomer

I'm starving

I'm seeking that which my soul yearns for; my loins burn sulfuric
brimstone - like flames in aim to lighten this desire
To feel it would be sublime, a mere rewind in time to which I aspire

I'm eager

I'm anticipating the experience of waking up in the clouds and lying down in the terrain
The shower of bliss upon my face; looking forward to glorious days

I'm hankering

As for now I'm flat-lined but my heart is waiting to beat again
When that time comes, relief will satisfy me and I shall praise Christ with a dance

I'm ravenous

I await the warmth from her hand upon my grace
The respect of her heart is my reward she grants my way

I'm rapacious

The touch from her lips upon mine own
The feeling of her utter surrender through her behavior
where the truth of her feelings is made known

I can't wait, I'm famished

The whisper given to me within my heart
Her respectfulness given through her essence and the fact that she hates to be apart

I'm esurient

Her confidence in her ability to please me repeatedly

In every way imaginable - she desires no other man or situation; we're one - she bleeds me

I'm voracious

Her thoughts are always placed on my well-being
Her excitement after a long day - she's happy just to see me

I'm thirsting

Her embrace of adoration I feel within her arms
During my time of depression or anxiety she rests not until she's found
a way to soothe me like the soothing power found in balm

I'm avid

I'm awaiting her protection of my confidence
The way she makes sure her actions with and without me
are those of loyalty and trustworthiness

I'm insatiate

Just waiting for the day where I would mean something to my beauty
The day where just me being alive is important to her; she proves it by her duties
I want to mean something to her as she will mean the world to me
I desire for us to share the blood of Christ in a connection thus spiritually
She awaits my presence each and everyday
She bows to the Lord of Grace in reverence; she realizes, and gives thanks
I love her and she loves me; no man can break the chains

We've bonded ourselves together the LOVE will always be displayed

I'm thirsty for this woman and this woman is hungry for me

LOVE is her name but her first name is Eternity

Selah!!!

The world versus the spirit

Love, in the Webster's Dictionary is defined as "strong affection for another arising out of kinship or personal ties; and or affection based on admiration, benevolence, or common interests (Merriam-Webster Dictionary)." The way in which the world portrays love is as an internally felt emotion that causes physiological responses externally. Allow me to explain; when a romance novel is written or a romance movie produced, the characters within claims to "fall in love," by which the audience is made privy to this information by what the character proclaims as well as how the character exudes his or her symptomatic physiological responses.

The love symptoms are usually the proverbial; "loss of appetite (can't eat), mental lapses in conventional thought (or can't think of anything else but the particular person), insomnia (can't sleep), abdominal fluctuations (butterflies), and heart palpitations (which is totally mental, feels like the heart skips a beat). The symptoms aforementioned do not begin to touch on the psycho-emotional feelings an individual claims during this time of "utter bliss." If this is true of what true love is, what happens when those feelings fade away? What happens when one begins to sleep again, eat again, think of other things besides the person whom he or she fell in love with; last, what happens when the individual's heart is back on rhythm? The issue here is those feelings are totally emotional and real love has to be, no, is more than an overly emotional, a-symptomatic experience. The truth is, these symptoms can be caused from lust just as it is assumed the feelings are caused by what this world believes to be love.

People carelessly throw the word around but has no idea what the word means. How is it that as a society, movies and romance novels have revealed to us true love? If this is the case (which is evident today) then true love can't and will never exist in the real experiential world. What we all need to know is that yes, when one first experiences love it is an overwhelmingly emotional phenomenon that cannot be fully explained. Love is like that; unexplainable at times. However, what happens when your spouse or significant other is constantly upsetting and or hurting you. Beloved let us turn attention to 1 Corinthians 13: 4-7 and the beginning of verse 8.

> Love is patient, love is kind. It does not envy, it does not boast, it is not proud. It does not dishonor others, it is not self-seeking, it is not easily angered, and it keeps no record of wrongs.

Love does not delight in evil but rejoices with the
truth. It always protects, always trusts, always
hopes, and always perseveres. Love never fails.
(1 Corinthians 13:4-8, NIV)

Beloved, this is spiritual love. This love is real; it is perfect.

Now the question remains, can real love exist in a humanistic
society? Logically speaking one would say no because this love
seems perfect, but is it? Is it asking too much for love to be
patient; meaning putting up with the one you deem worth the
time invested? Is it asking too much for love to be unselfish
toward the one you desire to constantly increase by decreasing
your own selfish gains? Is it wrong to desire to do right by your
significant other, never causing harm to them through evil
deeds or verbiage? Is it worth forgiving the person you adore,
not keeping records of his or her wrong doing? Ask yourself,
the one I am with or thinking of giving myself to; am I able
to forgive them for anything while protecting them with my
love? Ladies and gentlemen, if you answered yes to any one
of these questions, stop reading, pray about this situation in
your life, gather your belongings and peacefully walk away from
your unloving yet lust filled relationship. Continuing on in that
scripture reference, the beginning of verse eight says, "love
never fails," if you've answered yes to any of these questions, I
am sorry to inform you, but your love has failed. You are only
wasting your time.

SEEKING FANTASY

The intensity of the sun rays lessen as
the day comes to completion
The moon sets bright, burning and relinquishing
light, yet no heat is reaching
True love is difficult, in that it is rarely
distinguished, yet we're seeking
To feel its warmth like the sun, to be exploited under
its light like the moon, yet to live without sucks the
life out of you like blood from austere leaches

I'M SEEKING

Something surreal, un-heard of, abysmal in its
nature, pure and elite, something that causes
one to stumble over his or her speech
Something like a fantasy; veneration; an
essence only known to be obsolete;
Because the mere existence of such an
apparatus in its truest since couldn't be
Where trust rendezvous with homage of another's
essence, the clash contrives peace and tranquility

I'M STILL SEEKING

Selfishly I am leaving no stone unturned
to corral the emotion of love as I equally,
anticipate the action of its commitment

From it; I expect to get whatever I want, be

accepted, as I am with no carnal resentment

I seek the lovingly misconceptions of loves pleasures through

lust, one who is unafraid to brandish their willingness

To do whatever it takes for their love to be proven

accomplished, in me and still arrest respect

I need to be loved in a way no one else could annotate,

the love she has for me and how it resonates, within

my soul, as she faithfully adheres to my needs

She is incapable of being neglecting

My proclivity becomes hers as she has a need to

please me, make me happy, nurture me in such a way,

where righteousness is flaunted through her beauty

Wanting what's best for me, she gently, educates-to

me my insufficiencies', sooths my insecurities, my

ego she strokes with anticipated gratuity

To others she's misunderstood, they can't

place a finger on her inviolability

She's so committed to me, there is nothing

she won't do internally or externally

She's everything to me even when I to her I am nothing

I won't settle for less, this is my fantasy, seeking that which

Too many people are really living in LUST than in LOVE. The way in which society chooses to love today is juvenile. The world as it stands today knows nothing of love and because of it will and has faced consequences of lust. See, what society frequently finds itself involved in is settling. Wars have begun because of settling somewhere inhabitants weren't supposed to. Arguments, fights, feelings of anger, resentment, regret, doubt all stem from the mere fact that somewhere along the line settlement took place. Settling and love are two totally different concepts. To settle is to learn to coexist somewhere stumbled upon *(can anyone one say Christopher Columbus, the pilgrims and Indians)*. When one decides to settle, one has given up search for true serenity in a particular sought after territory.

As the world turns and society continues to increase in capacity, our settlement for a fabricated love, better known as lust, is and has become more prevalent. We have settled upon a superficial love that ejaculates sperm to create babies without fathers, and mothers with no education or purpose; when in fact, if real love exist today, when babies were born, fathers would be dad's and mothers would wait for REAL love to impregnate them with faith of love producing edible fruit forming a loving family.

My Heart Breaths

The wind swirls as I inhale, through my nostrils, breathes your name

Oxygen flows, as thoughts of you makes my dark
skin begin to glow, I feel no shame

Air fills my lungs, and blood in my veins, yet memories
of you, like a Slurpee, freezes my brain

My arteries pump, and my heart beats hard, as you've felt on your
back, the strong beat of my love that is often viewed as insane

My bones and joints loosen as my cerebral cortex gets to movin,
I'm choosing to write this to you for you to gain

Knowledge of how you cause my heart to beat and function
properly and how without you my pulse begins to fade

I'm not asking for you to stay but for you to know that for
you MY love was and is forever going to remain

My heart inhales as my thoughts impales my spirit as my soul
will stay in search of yours to finally become suitable mates

Just know wherever you go and whatever you do, TRUE love
is always here for you as it patiently awaits the day

When you realize the truth behind my words, matched by my actions,

the day you stop fighting the fact that OUR hearts breathe together

Until that day, IF, that day reveals the breath, for one another, OUR hearts take

---

Loving danger

The poem "Endangering Necessities" is hope that true love can exist in a humanistic society. It also exudes the commitment found in love. The truth is the poem speaks of how true love does and can exist; it displays the characteristics of and the possibility of true love. If people are patient, true love is inevitable. Loving another person is dangerous. However, society has decided to play it safe. Because of this, we have this promiscuous lifestyle of living to avoid heart break.

Love doesn't intentionally lie either. Before this is misunderstood look at it this way. Lying is a way of protecting. Unless a man or woman feels as though their partner is able to handle the truth, lying is the only option. However, for some, truth can be accepted. It hurts, but it can be handled. Truly loving someone means loving them in spirit and in truth. There is an issue with the truth however. When the truth is told, sometimes it's accepted as one would a lie. Why is this? If a man or woman finds you worthy of the truth why condemn them with your inability to accept it?

Lust is a fantasy, a mentally created phenomenon meant to stimulate an emotional response of something that is unreal. Because lust can take on the form of the same physiological responses love does, it can and is easily mistaken. Sex is lust, guys like to be told they're the greatest, they have a huge penis, and they know exactly how to please a woman; all lies. Truth is most guys are average size which by some article's I've read is only five and a half to six inches erected. Ladies, I'm sorry but this is anatomically correct, look it up. Furthermore, there is always going to be someone better than us – deal with it. Last, a man could never know how to please a woman unless a woman knows how to please herself (*and in turn shares that information unto men on how to do so*); so all men and women who base love on sexual relations as well as pure physical anatomy which is the description and mere definition of lust; I have two words for you...GROW UP!

Now what does all that have to do with being truthful? Well, again lying is like lust, it is a fantasy. If someone loves you enough to be real with you and operate a relationship based on reality and truth, he or she should not have to suffer the consequences because you are not spiritually, emotionally, and mature enough to live in reality. ***Real love exemplifies real forgiveness and forgiveness to a fault.*** I believe this is possible, only with the person in which you truly love.

Finally, we all know that the heart is a huge vascular muscle. Muscles are difficult to maintain. One has to constantly feed, nurture, care, and encourage the muscles for them to grow and to remain healthy. Protein shakes are vital because protein shakes provide the muscles with the nutrients needed to maintain the muscular intensity. The heart is like this; when one is able to walk into a room and his or her counterpart's heart feels uncharacteristically and medically impossibly strong enough to skip a beat yet still survive, that person's heart is strengthen by the mere presence of love.

CLOUD NINE AFFECTION

My mind doesn't allow me imagery
Outside of your descriptive silhouette

It is uncontrollable, my passion which resides inside of me
With each moment that passes, I hasten my
thoughts of you to what is next

Heavenly perception is what I can't repent
Affectionate foresight with you is what I won't neglect

How can I explicate what you mean to me in ways that relate?
To you for your own awareness, I take

Each moment with you as my last
My heart laughs around you; it elates

My soul is burning and yearning to be one with your person
Doubts are removed by your essence when it's lurking

Torn from your grasp leaves me empty
A void so deep as if parted like the red sea

Something like agape is this commitment I present unto you
Sacrificial in every way, more than emotional
soliloquies', these feelings remain knew

Even in its season the seasonings better when settled for a time
Reminiscent adjectives which define you
incinerates your name within mine mind

Higher than the heavens my heart floats like blown bubbles
A day without you is like death, dig my grave now – I'll get the shovel

Your worth is more than silver, gold can't pay for you
Mryth is sour and incense is stench when compared to you

I visualize only the best because I choose to be naïve
Even in your wrong doing, I'm naïve because I truly believe

You are fantastic, I'll blast it, and I'm speaking of your horn
You don't have to tute your own when you have me to form

The positive nature that is you I paint a near perfect picture
Hard to see imperfections when I'm concentrating
on me to be awesome for you in nature

My love for you can't even be solidified by the clouds
Beautifully conceived notions and ideas leaves
me yearning for you and proud

That you belong to me and I you as we sit above the 9th cloud

---

That presence of love is found in the one in which he or she has sought after his or her entire life. This is the one you need to hold on to, the one you dreamed about, had visions of, and prayed for. If you weren't able to see this person for a while, your love for this person would not die. No, on the contrary, it would increase because your heart would grow weak without him or her, so for a time life would be on pause until the one which one seeks returns to add that much needed protein shake for that muscle to maintain its intensity. When that intensity is observable again, oh what a feeling, co-workers see it, family, the church, and the community is made privy to this information of one's glow; it's true.

Now, most of what has been shared in this chapter has come in the form of relationship counseling. Because people failed to love, there is a failing economy. Lust actually drove us to this recessive economic disaster. Because love is not on the hearts of the few, the many have suffered and will suffer behind loves nemesis known as lust. This society has lusted its existence into oblivion. As a people, we got life morally, characteristically, socially, and spiritually twisted. The wars we've started, created, and fought in were behind lust. The social media phenomenon that has single-handedly destroyed face to face communication on this planet is a result of lust (if you don't believe-check out the Facebook and My space pages, nothing but lustful pictures, conversations, and idea's). Everything that once was has been destroyed by lust even while love was responsible for the creation of our mere existence. As a society, as a people, we have forgotten about love. Now we suffer the consequences of lust. Selah.

Life Without the Soul

I love her; I love him not

Have you ever loved someone so much that
you longed for them repeatedly?
Your mind cannot conceive a life
prior to or after this being
Your heart aches at the thought of another
holding them instead of you

Accomplishing things in your place;

even things you hate to do

I love him; I love her not

Does your love for them exceed their expectations?

Do you find yourself letting go with

them; freeing all inhibitions?

Do you believe in your heart that for

you it was God's intentions?

That the two of you would become one flesh;

speaking of the truth in God's creation

I love her; I love him not

I'm talking love that surpasses knowledge

that is merely perceived

A love so precious it seems impossible to believe

A fantasy is what others would say upon gazing

upon you and the love in which you cleave

Passion so great, indeed, it causes your soul to bleed

I love him; I love her not

The truth is no one can replace the

presence of the their essence

The mere sight of this person is

defeated by another's advances

Your vision is set solely upon the soul

in which your soul mates

No one could ever create in you the joy

in what your true sweets taste...

In which your hearts fluids permeates

The nectar found in true love in him, in

her – you've realized your fates;

Your spirits relate

I love her; I love him not

The sum of all fears is the abhorrence

of living without this person

To get out of bed without them next to

you requires a heart surgeon

Because your heart is broken; and sorrow starts lurking

The genre of music changes within your cognitive

processes as the mood change approaches

I love him; I love her not

The mere thought of this person makes

you want to modify insufficiencies

Things about yourself that causes the one you love to flee

You realize selflessness should in

this case always supersede

The selfishness in you as you understand

the power of his or her needs

There is nothing in this world that could ever equal

The importance this person brings to

life, you dream of the steeple

The day the two becomes one you're done with seeking

A mate, because your soul is satisfied with this

being's character, without them life is meaningless

I love him; I love her not

IT'S FAIR TO SAY I LOVE HIM; I LOVE HER

The discussion continues; do you know what love is? What would be your definition?

Are we as people capable of love?

Chapter 5

Prude Promiscuity

Socialistic interaction proves that times have changed, are changing, and will continually change; and based on factual evidence seen from day – to – day reciprocation; this kind of change is not for good but unfortunately bad.

Let us face today's truth, sex is everywhere and is in everything. Advertisement is often one of the major contributors to sexual innuendos in the media today. Sex, the best thing since sliced bread yet the worst consequence in a heat of passion. The truth about sex is, it is exciting in the beginning, but begins to become prude and more lame with repetition. Sex, a known hot commodity, can also be known as the very phenomenon which made and or makes the relationship cold. What happens in marriages today is that sex freezes the very core of the commitment between two individuals. How is it that sex brings individuals together, yet in the end, is often responsible for tearing one another apart? The answers are simply complicating, meaning the answers are clear but the solutions are incompatible with the selfish nature of mankind.

The fire that once burned in the bedroom is often put out by the cold ice of prude behavioral trends which leads to intimacy issues. Intimacy issues come in various forms. According to an excerpt, found on www.psychpage.com named *Relationship Reasons for Divorce*, "20-25% of mediation groups say an affair was a reason, but the reason given by 80% is deterioration of intimacy." 80% is a staggering percentage. And still, Dr. William H Doherty revealed in his essay, *How common is divorce and what are the reason's*, a national survey declares 55% of marriages end because of infidelity.

One could safely assume that repetition created boredom and boredom birth curiosity which born of curiosity came infidelity. Simply put, it got boring in the bedroom. Couples were/are afraid to spice things up. Children took up time that used to be rip the clothes off, get down and dirty time. But for some, the number one reason infidelity arose or even became a possibility, is because of what one would not do, chose not to do, and refused to try in the bedroom. Check out this excerpt which is the true deep dark desires carried by most humans but for some reasons are afraid to display, express, or commit behind closed doors.

SHUTTERING ANIMALISTIC DARKNESS

I find myself having to hold back in
intense moments of intimacy
So much is built up within me
If one could view my internal cognitive
processes, from me they'd flee
My physiological extremities react intently to that which
is filled with deep dark desires; down-right shuttering
To my core, ravaging curiosity concerns me as
to what the purpose of such planted seed
Then I think
Within me there is a certain calignosity
Rage, plus lust, divided by emotions; a dose proven lethally

For me, it is not enough to be inside of you
It is not enough to merely ask of you
To share with me who's your body belongs to
Only for you to tell me something you
may have told another dude
NO!
I must display to you through fierce interaction
That you belong to ME and my
ownership through satisfaction

Domination is a trait owned by this man
It is why I'd rather do what I want without limitations

I want to subdue you and make you cry out
Pull you close to me, grabbing your extremities with force,
proceeding to leave marks on you from my mouth
Have a hand full of hair slowly yet painfully
thrusting with my hand over your mouth
Can't wake the children love, you're getting a bit loud!

I don't need or want to speed
I WILL have you feel ALL of me
I want to feel your arteries pulsate between my teeth
I will have you scream; but only in ecstasy
Ever had a man lift you up in his arms
while tenderizing your meat?
Then tossing you on your back grabbing
your throat pounding without cease?
Slightly choking you in intimacy YOU BELONG TO ME!
Folding you like a pretzel, I want to test how deep
My depth could reach

My hands will reach around to the back of your neck
You will taste what it is I have left
I won't try to choke you but I want to test your throat flex
A gag of encouragement as your mouth continues to stretch

I am just...
So animalistic ally darkened by my thought process

I'm sorry if I am offending you
I'm just trying to make sure I educate you
I hold back something fierce because I
don't want to frighten you
But regularity dipped in the norm is not something I am into

After you taste this deep dark chocolaty sweetness
Your face dripping with cream filling,
I beseech your weakness
Exotic confusion I can see your bewilderment
How you just allowed yourself to be totally dominated
Just as you think it was over
I'm coming to kiss you on your shoulder

Sliding my hands in-between your thighs
I pick you up – upside down eating your American pie
Blood rushing to your head and mine
Again you find me between your lips deep inside
Again tossed upon the couch you define
What you feel, you say you love me and I'm
Even more turned on; you've said the magic words
Inside you my hand's acting as a verb
My tongue is now knocking at the back door

Your surprise is elevated by your clench
I whisper to you I will have my way
trust me and don't be tense
Lubrication supplied you can't understand why you went
Along with this - but for some reason I'm
the man you just can't relent with
Softly and tenderly I break the walls of normality
The rules of engagement broken by
lovingly lustful intensity
You find enjoyment of going against societal rules
You relaxed and felt pleasure you're
giving yourself to US and to you

Liberation!

Painfully Pleasurable I'm taking it slow but still
taking you by force with my other hand
Which fills the other glory hole as your face shows
so much pleasure; it seems too much to stand!
I'm pulling your hair back telling you - you belong to me
You submit with no denials so willingly
You speed up as your happiness hardens
getting ready to explode
I toss you on top of my face waiting for that precious load

Totally nasty yet very pleasurable am I
But my love is driven by my animalistic ways
No doubt this is areas filled with shades of gray
I will leave marks, I will make you scream
Blood may flow, but all in ecstasy
Darkness rises as my nature does frequently
At the thought of the deep dark things it seems
Believe me, this is only the beginning
Of my darkest thoughts that are
animalistic ally shuttering!!!
To be continued ...

Now, in no way is infidelity being given a pass. The people who cheat on spouses should be held responsible; infidelity is not being overlooked here at all. However, one suggests that infidelity could be prevented if and only IF both individuals are willing to indulge in freedom of expression in the bedroom. Things like anal sex, oral sex, toys, food, handcuffs, ropes, swings, and so - on should not be frowned upon but rather freely accepted and applauded. When two people (speaking from a marriage standpoint honestly) come together, pleasure and the way to induce it upon one another should never be seen as shameful or embarrassing, rather shameless and an honor to please. One would argue that every intimate moment in a marriage should be pornographic in nature every time the two shares flesh. Ladies, if he wants to, allow him to cum on your face or in your mouth and enjoy it. Men, if she wants you to, lick her butt hole, allow her to squirt her juices on your face, or allow her the opportunity to sit on your face. Be open and free with one another. It will take the power away from infidelity. Another growing issue for some reason; women will do all kinds of crazy things before they are married with various guys, but as soon as she marries, all of a sudden her last name becomes Mrs. Prude. Why?

The aforementioned poem expresses the freedom of sexual expression. Although these are just words to most, one feels as though there is no reason why this kind of intimacy should be deemed unusual or abnormal. A large percent of dysfunction in relationships and or marriages is the selfish notion to hold back from one another what each person deserves. The Holy bible even says that the two should not withhold from one another accept by mutual consent for a time of prayer and fasting. Factually speaking, the apostle Paul states in 1 Corinthians 7, *"Do not deprive each other except perhaps by mutual consent and for a time, so that you may devote yourselves to prayer. Then come together again so that Satan will not tempt you because of your lack of self-control* (1 Corinthians 7:5, NIV)." The woman deserves every nerve to be tingled, every smell to have a scent of sensual pleasure, every touch to be shatteringly sensitive, every taste to be lustfully consuming, every moan to be genuinely exacerbating, and every sight to be indulgingly appeasing.

However, for some men, getting his (his euphoric ejaculation) is more important than her feeling loved, appreciated, desired, and for some women, quantity has taken precedence over quality. Somewhere along the lines the two never really became one flesh, biblically speaking. To become one flesh is to share in each other's emotions, desires, pleasures, curiosities, fears, fantasy, and most of all Spirit. Alas, what society has done is bewildered the minds of the individual so much so that the individuals are incapable of selfless acts of pleasure. As society would have it, quantity given at a fast pace is normal and yet beneficial; quality, given at a slow pace is abnormal yet impossible. Women began lying to men so much, and men to women, that when a time of bliss is shared, questions are dividing one's thoughts to dread and awful doubt. Why? Because these days, there seems to be no truth in loving making: a very few can say that they have had free, intimate, lustful, love making sessions...

Intimate whisper

I find it hard to believe
That in a moment of passion you actually believe what you say
This is why I'd rather be in love before I proceed
In fierce intimacy, because of my ability,
to make your body scream
Lustfully

I'm recalling the moments of ecstasy
The moment I had you in a trance, your body
shivering, my hands caressing thee
You were speechless at first, but the pleasure got worse
In a instance your back jerked; upward,
you backed up into me
In a moment you whispered interesting soliloquies
Lustfully

Softly, I canvassed you in a flash of heat...
How I felt to you - and you replied after
minutes of gritting your teeth
You proclaimed I was the best and there was no one else
That has ever made you feel this way...
In an instant I smiled cognitively, my mind was at ease
I'm pleasing her, don't stop, proceed
Lustfully

I made sure to take my time
I wanted to be inside of your mind
Being inside of you wasn't enough — I had
to imprint upon your imagination
It was my duty to guide you to a place of sublime
With a hand full of your hair, you
murmured out you loved me
Lustfully

I asked you how much

As I began with gripping your thighs with a masculine tough touch

Concentrating on controlling my intensity

You said in a moment of breathlessness -

how so much, you adored me

My excitement was enticing, I sped up aggressively

Lustfully

Pain was written all over your face

I stopped to make sure that you were ok

You begged, don't stop; pain is pleasure - is what they say

The thought of harming you in my

mind, I continued without haste

Stunned still by the breathless words you proclaimed

Lustfully

Deeper and deeper I penetrated your gender

Biting your neck, pulling you close, I

felt your eminent surrender

At one point I felt you give yourself totally to us

To soften and nurture you, I tasted you with no fuss

A kiss to remind you of my passionate love

You grabbed the back of my head, your

tongue you dominantly shoved;

In my mouth

Lustfully

Intensely you're kissing me

Whispering how much you need me

How much life would be incomplete without my being

You begged for me to never leave you, not

to forsake what we are building

You cry with joy, as your climax was approaching

You shout my name at my command

Lustfully

The time has passed and now we are cuddling

I'm rubbing your hair, your back, while I am listening

To your heart's speed, the thumps I hear are pounding

I'm left wondering if what you really

revealed meant anything

You lean over and kiss me and reassure I'm the greatest thing

To ever happen to you, but I can't help thinking

Was it real or was it just something...

We tend to whisper while in a moment of intimacy

Lustfully

Is there truth in love making?

The ugly truth is, if moments like these are being shared between persons, it is not the individual's person he or she is sharing this climactic experience with. The ugly truth is today, there are still women who will not put a penis in her mouth; today there are men who will not wiggle his tongue on a vagina. Today foreplay is instituted to be substituted from that which was created for the consummation of two becoming one body! Foreplay is at its nature a pretense of nastiness which leads to the main meal of sexual penetration. Shame in a long and committed relationship should never be a recipe to doubt and selfishness because there is nothing shameful of a woman putting aside her notion of what a lady should be and accepting the role of a bonafide whore to secure in her husband a long and satisfying marriage. Ladies, the truth is every man wants a woman to take home to mom, it is better said, a LADY in the streets and a FREAK in the BED. Men, don't be afraid to be your woman's gigolo. What is wrong with performing acts that only paid prostitutes do? If it is wise, he or she should remember, what one won't do, the other most assuredly will!

A time forgotten is true monogamy. Today, good sex can only be experienced when multiple parties are involved. Various vaginal escapades bred the phrase; there is nothing better than pussy but new pussy." With that type of mentality, there will be a failure on her part to open up and share with you some of the fantasies in which she frequently visits in her mind, except it is not her failure, but the man's because she cannot trust you will protect her body monogamously. Women, you talk so much about size, I can remember a time when that was not so important, but rather, the way he felt for you, or the way he touched you and made you feel. Society today has hijacked sex for promiscuous prudeness and superficial overindulgence.

Let us converse of the matters of sex:

What will you do or not do for the sake of that person dearest to you?

Do you have limits? Should you have limits with your spouse?

Why does the sexual freedom discontinue with marriage?

Chapter 6

Socialistic Constriction

Socialistic interaction proves that times have changed, are changing, and will continually change; and based on factual evidence seen from day – to – day reciprocation; this kind of change is not for good but unfortunately bad.

The art of conversation is now a thing of the past and we only have ourselves to blame. Why? In an adolescent attempt to remain connected and to fill voids that can only be filled by one's acknowledgement of a need of something bigger, stronger, higher than one's self, we have given in to the sin of social media. That's right! I said it! Social media is the devil that has tempted, constricted, offended, and dismembered the art of conversation; the human relationship; and the intelligence of mankind. I stand by my words.

Look at what society have become. Men no longer are taught by men to be men because father's are not sitting down with the young seeds planted, watering the seed properly; nurturing the seed to become a tree of life, which provides fresh air through naturally generated oxygen; a tree which provides shade and protection from a harsh environment. A strong tree which provides everyday provisions in one way or another is now forgotten; it is now a tree of the past. A father's affections are no longer in the seed but rather in the planting of seeds in the wrong type of fields or gardens found in a spoiled meat market of social media. The willingness to turn off the computer and hand held devices to impart wisdom to society's next generation is gone. Social media has stolen our men and manhood today. What is viewed and seen on Facebook is training our men of tomorrow in the way in which he should go. The sad trend is the same could and should be said for the young women of tomorrow. Social media has hijacked integrity and the moral code of ethics.

Look at the state in which we find spouses, significant others, etc. What ever happened to men being men? You know, the man who sought out his wife by first meeting her face to face, conversing with her verbally and not by email; or by punching in the alphabet with his thumbs to form sentences better expressed by the human tongue spoken through the mouth which protects his speech. What happen to the testosterone to go and seek his mate, court her properly, winning her over with chivalrous methods which promised respect, and having the boldness to display his interest by speech led with action? The answer is simple and it is seen daily through socialistic interactions. Men now hide behind the internet to meet his bride. He is not man enough to seek out his wife but rather takes the easy route and searches the internet for her. Just remember, mail ordered is mail ordered and is not authentic but fast food. Fast food is bad for you and in the end your digestive system will become tainted by some form of fabricated meat injected with non-sense just for the food to be preserved.

Women on the other hand are allowing men to behave like sheepish, shy young boys. Women aren't requiring men to be men. Women are so enamored with words they overlook the behaviors suggesting she should leave him alone in order that he may mature. The most infuriating thing is how women cry and complain about boys when she herself did not seek a man!!! Ladies, if you allow yourself to be swept off your feet by the internet and or social media, you deserve everything that comes with that atrocity. You too can savor the taste of a home cooked meal but you as well settle for fast food and thus receive fast results. Selah. Both women and men need to be more mature in his or her search and dealings with the opposite sex. Men seek women, let the boys seek girls. Women seek men, let the girls receive boys. Get off the social media and return to the days of prominence. Seek your spouse without the internet. Women allow your knight to come and retrieve you, be parents and stop allowing television and Facebook to raise your children. Bring back the days when families were created with all the proper ingredients of a home cooked meal and not with the tainted preservatives of today's fast food.

Identity theft

Society has forgotten what and who it is. Our identity is now found in the numerical language. What is meant is this; society has exchanged face to face interactions with computer generated exchanges of idea's and forethought. Whatever we as humans have been named by our parents; we renamed ourselves with code names, or should it be said, "screen names" and or nick names. The identity of the human race was lost the moment social media began. It should not be the blame of social media's inventors for the cause of humanities fall from grace. As a fact, social media was not created for the usage that is seen today.

The thought of reaching loved ones from across the nations was and is one of the greatest ideas of this century. When Facebook, twitter, and other social programs are used properly; to promote communication across nations, to participate in cultural movements around the world, to gain access to current events in and around other nations, and to assist in the educational and business promotional needs in and around our society, it is deemed a program worthy to be an illuminated source of social movement. However, social media is not used in this way. Social media is nothing more than the cyber meat market of today. It is nothing more than a hook up sight with inappropriate, idiotic, sexual deviancy, lewd behaviors and speech where the most ignorant of people of various stereotypical backgrounds come to conform together. Social media is your modern day night club of today. Again, our identity has been taken by this pretentious and arrogant program. People who are reminiscent of a time past where folks behaved with decency and respect to one's self as well as others have suffered greatly through these perilous times.

What shall we as a society say about the way in which we've allowed ourselves to be identified by social media? Should we not be ashamed of what has become of us? Should there be no embarrassment of whence we once came to where we have gone and to who we've become? Once identified as the nation from whence freedom of expression through poetic notation, and well educated speech was heralded, we now have become identified as the nation who is one of the lowest in education and morally bankrupt (*and this is just the Unites States*). The moment society substituted full thought out and thought provoking sentences with the new "text language" in which abbreviations are made to form full thoughts and ideals to form half-witted, fragment sentences, is the very moment we lost who we were. Whereas society used to be thought of or identified as a straight forward, ever progressive society moving towards enlightenment; even with today's technology, we've returned to an age of buffoonery. It is as if the industrial revolution had never taken place. The age of the Flinstone's seems back in effect. The time has long passed when the people of society held thought provoking dialogue. To hear what the conversation's are today is to hear grown adults sound like that of adolescent children speaking about subjects likened to what is on the Cartoon Network!

Conversations today consist of that which expels it way from a donkey's anus releasing toxins cleaning the animals system. What society should do is expel these kinds of conversation from within itself to preserve that which is still decent of us today. Conversations like, what's going on with the housewives of Atlanta, what happened in last week's episode of Jersey Shore's, or what happened with Jay Z and Beyonce, what do you think about that new Drake album, what party is happening this weekend, did you see what so and so posted on Facebook, and don't forget the business of celebrity's society seems to eat up. Everyone is concerned about who is sleeping with who, who said what on Facebook, where the next party is going to be and so-on; it is utterly ridiculous. Now wonder why society is at a stand – still, everyone seems so vain! It's disgusting! Society has restricted any forms of education, art, and real music, along with social issues and mobility from all conversations and this is who we are today.

Once upon a time, the patrons of society used to dictate to the media what was displayed. Now it seems that the media dictates to the patrons what will be shown or heard through the media's frequencies. It should be found shameful what we as a society accept today. To regain what was lost, the television should be shut off, the radio burned at the stake, and the engine which is social media should be shut down if we desire to save what is left of our society. Forward movement will only occur when the civilians of this world step up and demand something better, something intellectual, something worth the time re-learning again, the art of conversation and every good fruit born from it.

Substituted

Good day to you, how do you do this day?
Simple right, it starts with the
God – given breath of life
Inhale, allow your thoughts to form for one
second; you got it, it is time to ignite
As you exhale, allow your mind to be at ease
Display your intelligence, search his mind,
search her heart for the important things
Allow him allow her to see
Your interest lies beyond what
you're gazing upon physically
**What is your name? Where are you
from? If you don't me asking....**

A time ago this was the ice breaker which
sparked flames to a long lasting unity
Individuals became one from tantalizing
conversation which was led by certain continuity
It was an art of one's true integrity, and
his or her ability to just speak
Speaking is no longer a part of the human dialect
These days are filled with thoughtless
postings, emails, and ambiguous texts
The personalization where souls match
through the eyes have been replaced
These days of meeting are happening via
Facebook, no longer through warm embrace
What brings you this way? What do you do?
Our thumbs speak in our place we've
forgotten how to conversate
Full sentences are of past tense, today
we allow fragments to compensate
For the lack of knowledge and the respect that
comes with attempting to learn of a person
Cowardly speaking with confidence through
a screen; hiding true intentions with
indiscretion on the brain just lurking
Personality is lost because the
media is speaking for us

Socially defeated we've allowed

our fingers to destroy us

We should exchange numbers and

maybe have dinner. I find you

interesting and need to know more

We've fallen subject to suspect

postings and texts; we neglect

The human need to socialize while we

debate through enticing intellect

What we speak of often is superficiality with

broadened vain conceit as we breathe sex

We wonder why hearts are left broken and

a society left to ruins; it's because we led

the conversation via posting and or text

It was a pleasure speaking with you

Selah!!!

Chapter's End

Opinionated

Over and over I've told myself that this excerpt was that of mine own thoughts; things I think of everyday. See, I'm a thinker; there are puzzles within my mind that I am constantly and desperately trying to solve. I have these conversations hoping that by the end of the dialogue between my two ears, I would have suitable suggestions and logical explanations to solve the ominous and bewildering behavioral trends humans continue displaying this present day. This task is challenging. Yet, as I have written various poems, excerpts, and explanations therein, illumination occurs as I now realize that these are not just mere thoughts of mine, but are additionally extensive, distinctive, distinguished and unique beliefs I carry and am holding to be part of my moral compass.

I'm quite traditionalistic yet very eclectic in my approach to life. When it comes to faith, family, love, and marriage, I fall in the old traditional approach. However, when it comes to creative thought, music, art, individualism and various topics therein, I find myself to be pretty eclectic (out of the box); which leads me to my reasons for the various sections of this text.

Men and women

Ultimately, the belief is that there is a man who finds his bride and loves her unconditionally. His love is traditionally displayed by the work he does outside the house. He also displays this love by imparting wisdom to his children and yes, even to his wife. He makes sure his house is provided for and he is the leader of his home. He leads his family spiritually first and physically second; he's the example on how to live life even through life's difficulties. He manages home with love, not with an iron fist. He is the example to his children; to his son he is the male role model to follow; to his daughter, he is the man she hopes to marry. He is the one who makes the final decision for his home (after he has heard the council of his wife). He works and provides in various ways, not just physically or monetarily but emotionally and always most importantly spiritually. However, men today are just plain ignorant to the type of man he should be. The world would have men to believe that making the big bucks, accruing nice things along with a huge house makes him manly, while some men care not to work at all; men are just NOT men.

Men seem to be an example of some pre-pubescent momma's boy, who allows his woman to do the working in and out of the home for him. The issue with men today is there are no real men raising men; women are attempting to. The most egregious statement I've heard a woman say is, "I'm the momma and the daddy." Yes, it is usually black women running around beating her own breast as if she really has a penis swinging between her legs. Women (black or white), understand this, just because you have done what you were supposed to do in raising your child, albeit on your own or whatever have you, doing so does not make you a man and most definitely not the father. Please in the name of the most-high God, stop repeating that non-sense to your children. It does not sway them nor does it help your cause whatever that may be.

Women are supposed to be elegant treasures; fine gold sheltered within the confines of an expensive jewelry box. She, by historical account is, loving, kind, and gentle. She is submissive to a capable man and yet strong enough to walk alongside of and not in front of her spouse. She is very intelligent. She walks with honor and carry's herself with respect. Her love is displayed by what she does inside of the home. She is (yet no longer) loyal, faithful, and dependent upon her husband. She gave herself on the day she proclaimed "I do" and not every time someone displayed interest or said "hello" with a smile. She was dependable and reliable. She gave great advice and assisted her husband in everything while supporting him in the same manner. Her reputation was impressive and her commitment

to her family, undeniable. She was a queen, yet not the self -
proclaimed one (which usually means she's not when she has to
constantly remind people). Just like the man however, women
are hard to find. To date, we have had an overwhelming influx
of females running rampant in society.

The females are rude, loud, abrasive, nasty and promiscuous.
She is influenced by her friends and easily swayed by what this
world says she should be. She spreads her legs and opens her
mouth to any guy who seems interested momentarily and or
says a few nice words; she's so shallow. There is no chase with
today's female, she is easy to have and easy to discard. Her vain
conceit leads her to not only disruptive speech but a destructive
perception of life as well. She stands for nothing and reality
television is her accountability partner. She's irresponsible;
putting any man above her children. She is so confused she
actually believes that she is the man of the house though one
is present. She's sad; she leaves nothing to the imagination in
terms of her appearance. She only thinks of herself and has the
persistent need to be seen and heard. Her mind is adolescently
driven and she herself is a waste of space. There's nothing special
about her. Her reputation is weary and displayed all over social
media. She's known not as a wife or even wife material but a
friend to have fun with and she accepts this and takes that
description as a compliment. She's just a friend with benefits;
there is nothing special to her at all.

Individualism

Individuality is definitely a concept of the past. People today are so busy trying to fit into this unfortunate existence known as society, that he or she has forgotten the concept of "self." Society is defined by movements. For instance, whatever subject, issue, or trends presently happening at any particular time in the environment, the individuals within will collectively conform to identify with, and thus become just like one another. Examples of this can be seen with the LGBT movement, the election of the first young black president, Islamic extremism, also recognized as a new phenomenon or movement, and things as small as tattoo's, piercings, drug use and alcohol abuse, along with promiscuity. These are clear examples of a society adapting and conforming to a label or identity known as the "**IN**" crowd (whether you see these things bad or good is of no importance). This occurrence is accompanied by a similar fear held by the individuals within the aforementioned habitat.

The new and ferocious fear that has arisen amidst various communities today is known as originality; simply put, being one's self or the fear of being different. Saddening to realize that society is now without original thinkers. The timeline between history and the present day is fading with the tapping of each key it takes to write this manuscript which carries the disappointing cognizance that originality is a phenomenon of the past. Society will starve without the creative cognitive processes of those of an original mind. If we as a society choose not to stand up and cry aloud for those originals to arise and take his or her rightful place amongst us, the abhorrent reality is our future is non-existent. What does this mean?

A rebirth is needed. Every young black man does not need to presume that he is an athlete, rapper, singer, dancer, or some kind of entertainer. Knowledge is power; yet instead of seeking power, young black men seek easy money, relying on whatever talent he thinks he has to be "successful." He does not realize that he is being placed on display and is signing a promissory note of ownership to the organization or people selling him for what he has to offer (until that entity uses everything he has and is). Sounds a lot like slavery does it not? The truth is, this is all a ploy to keep young black men out of wall-street, out of the corporations, and yes, out of the government (they would call it public service). However, this too is a conversation for another manuscript.

The media has to restore the hope and the faith in education, where it leads, rather than lies and smoke screens of quick fixes and literal hoaxes to success. The media should stop portraying successful black men only as entertainer's for society's households while young black men should start to look past the media for ideas on success and or mentors to follow. This institution should be real and explain that the results seen on television are not usual. Read the fine print please! A regeneration of truth needs to be unveiled so that we can promote originality and cease with the subjective lies of conformity.

In the same way, young women need to understand that not every beautiful woman is a size one or two; nor does she have to open her legs to everyone so that she can experience some level of success; not every woman succeeded this way. Media lies and the stereotypical nature this institution deals in has become a reason why we have become a nation, **NO**, a world forgotten and greatness stalled. Society as a whole needs to look past what is on the television for our world to experience a real and true objective change.

Musical forethought

A time ago music was used as a release of various kinds of emotions. As mentioned in the text, music was a way in which each member of society could escape harsh realities of life. In addition, music was also a way in which one could illuminate the current state of affairs within a given environment. Music at one time or another meant something. One could feel music; one could breathe music; it is safe to say that music was life and life was music. However, as the years passed by, society has witnessed the change from albums to eight tracks, eight tracks to cassette, cassette to CD and now CD's to mp3 or digital downloads, and music has found itself on life support.

Music will die soon. The once talented and intelligent individuals who wrote, composed, and delivered music through talented and beautiful voice are now engulfed by the aforementioned peer individualist. Yes, it is true; music has been handed over to idiotic, gimmick - filled, illiterate simpleton's who know nothing of real music. All music to date sounds exactly the same. Musical genre's does not exist any longer. House music (formerly known as techno) has flooded all genres while pop is the new undertone and it's all smothered under the rear-end of hip-hop. The lyrics are rudimentary and they too are sounding similar. Will someone please just pull the plug already? It is like watching a loved one suffering from a terminal illness. The only thing one can do is pull the plug and allow our love to rest in peace.

The blame could easily be put on the music industry as a whole. However, if we are honest we ourselves are to blame. The moment the industry allowed ignorance and gimmicks into the fray we should have stood up in an uproar and demanded respect and honor to be restored. Instead, we laughed it off as something cute and different while silently supporting the idiotic production of music with our monetary offerings. The crap we hear on the radio is due in large part to our inability to stand and be original. Music today is what conformity looks like. Education in society is down, culture is overlooked, stupidity is celebrated, ignorance is bliss, and promiscuity is valued over a good reputation. Music is a direct representation of who we have become as a people. Enough said!!!

Love or is it lust

Ask 100 people what love is and you'll more than likely hear contrasting answers. How can love be explained? Is it possible to truly understand love? Are humans capable of defining love in its truest sense? People today have proven to be incapable of comprending such a phenomenon as love. The reason for this ignorance is because of the way in which society uses the word love. The word love in society is often used as a noun, being that a noun is a person, place, thing or idea. What happens is this word is used as an emotional explanation versus a behavioral commitment. The word love is actually a verb, meaning love is and can only be explained by what a person does versus what he or she says. A commitment that is defined by its sacrificial behavioral trends is the only way one can define love. However, the understanding is skewed because the word is overly uttered in times of playschool passion and puppy dog emotions. What people often feel is lust, not love.

Lust is often misconstrued as love because of the way love is used in music and speech today. What is lust? Most dictionaries define lust as a strong emotion or feeling. This is exactly how the word love is used today. The problem is people feel something strong and automatically go to the word love without knowing the meaning. Ladies, when a man says that he loves you check his actions. If you're sick, is he attempting to take care of you? In what way is he willing or does he sacrifice for you? Desires come and go, so what exactly happens when one begins to lose that desire for another? The human specie's will not always be desirable. Our bodies will break down and our looks will fade. Our attitudes will change and our mental state will be shaken. What then? Again, ask yourself is it love, or is it lust.

The bedroom

This section of the compendium should be prefaced with the explanation that this particular subject is speaking of married people alone (as singles have various styles and views on single). With that being stated, what is the issue with sex and marriage? Why does it seem, especially from men's point of view, intimacy automatically decreases with the ring of commitment? One could argue that divorce is running rampant because of this very issue. Bewildering is the term one would use to define this on-going phenomenon. Excuse the speech that follows but a woman, before she decides to get married, is looser than a size 12 pants on a woman who is naturally a size 3. Why is this? Women have a whore type personality before marriage. Yet when she marries she becomes a holy nun. Before marriage a woman will suck, lick, screw, and be just as nasty as the females in pornos; and with various men!!!! Before marriage a woman will suck start a leaf blower!!! Friends with benefits seem more NEW and EXCITING supposedly. However, new and unknown leads to STD's and excitement can and should be double in marriage with the freedom and comfort of knowing this person most intimately.

The struggle is real. Ladies, if you desire to hold on to your marriage, the same whore you were as a friend, you should be double as a wife. Marriage is meant to be for life. If a slut is what you want to be don't get married; just be a slut. Trust that no one will judge you till after he or she is done with you. Why in the world would a spouse do this to another? It is true, it is not just women doing this, however it is more heard of with women than with men. Marriage is not an agreement of celibacy but rather God says a time in which the two "become one flesh," meaning consummate the marriage with the physical acts of love. What will happen undoubtedly is infidelity on both sides if society continues to get this issue backwards. Sexual freedom should not be for the un-married, but for the individuals who took an oath to fulfill each other's needs until death with the blessing of God. More could be said about this subject but this could be furthered within a different manuscript.

End game

What it comes down to is dignity, respect, honor, pride and most of all love. We were a society that once enjoyed the enlightenment education, love of culture and love of people once brought us. We celebrated decorated members of society who would have held the label, creative or enlightened originals. Of course, he or she was not originally accepted until his or her work was put on display. Yes, even these people were deemed abnormal; however, those abnormalities were the cause of our forward movement. Look at the result of these people who were deemed abnormal or strange; cures to illnesses were created, books written which taught us about our anatomy and cognitive processes, art created and displayed, music composed and used as therapy, bridges built, communities constructed, eyes opened to life and the spoils which were the result of blessings of the true birth of enlightenment. Positives (although America has many negative truths) were born of the past. Now what can we say in our future about the present day in which we find ourselves if we don't find our way back?

The detail of this compendium explicates everything erroneous with the cognitive processes of the human mind today. The thoughts held by the human specie's are faulty from the start of development, thus leading to asinine behavior. The various poems and scripts are artistic manuscripts dictated with the sole purpose to provoke and persuade while enlightening the reader on the very real issues within this place we call society. The love we once held as a society with one another as well as the love of culture is gone while the new era of selfishness, greed, and again vain conceit is slowly destroying us. This book is written through the essence and allure of poetry to reveal the art once lost. We need re-creation...we need rejuvenation!

This conversation is also useful as a pre-courting or pre-dating informational guide. The issue with relationships is people are constantly pretending and or promulgating a product of his or herself that is fallacious advertisement. By reading this book, one could retrieve some insight as to what the opposite sex feels, what he or she believes, as well as his or her character.

Life was defined by how we lived; but now how we live defines our life and the society that has and may very well be known as everything forgotten.

I pray you got the message. IT IS TIME FOR A SOCIAL REVOLUTION.

Let us get it started with the conversation!
God bless. Grace and peace

References

"Game". Merriam-Webster Online. (n.d.). Received from:
http://i.word.com/idictionary/game

Hawkins, A.J., PH.D.& Fackell, T.A., J.D.().Should I Keep trying
to work it out: A guidebook for individuals and couples at the
crossroads of divorce (and before). Chpt 3.

"Love". Merriam-Webster Online. (n.d.). Retrieved from:game
http://i.word.com/idictionary/love

Myers, D. (2008). *Social Psychology* 9th.ed.

"Relationship Reason for Divorce". Psychpage.com. Retrieved from:
http://www.psychpage.com/family/mod_couples_thx/divorce.html

Holy Bible: New International Version. (2011). Grand Rapids, Mich.:
Zondervan.

About the Author

Sir John Hawkins, the only male within his family to graduate High school and awarded multiple college degrees with his prized being in Psychology. He writes as one born of six children and life experiences; which in his mind believes, "life is poetic." He is continuing education in Theology/Christian Counseling.